THE BROADVIEW
Introduction to
Literature

Literary Non-fiction

THE BROADVIEW
Introduction to
Literature

Literary Non-fiction

General Editors
Lisa Chalykoff
Neta Gordon
Paul Lumsden

broadview press

Library and Archives Canada Cataloguing in Publication

    The Broadview introduction to literature, literary non-fiction / general editors, Lisa Chalykoff, Neta Gordon, Paul Lumsden.

Includes index.
ISBN 978-1-55481-180-9 (pbk.)

    1. English essays. 2. American essays. 3. Canadian essays (English). 4. Creative nonfiction, English. 5. Creative nonfiction, American. 6. Creative nonfiction, Canadian (English). 7. Reportage literature, English. 8. Reportage literature, American. 9. Reportage literature, Canadian (English). 10. Creative nonfiction—Translations into English. I. Chalykoff, Lisa, editor of compilation II. Gordon, Neta, 1971-, editor of compilation III. Lumsden, Paul, 1961-, editor of compilation IV. Title: Introduction to literature, literary non-fiction.

PN6141.B76 2013   808.84   C2013-903882-5

Broadview Press is an independent, international publishing house, incorporated in 1985. We welcome comments and suggestions regarding any aspect of our publications—please feel free to contact us at the addresses below or at broadview@broadviewpress.com.

North America	PO Box 1243, Peterborough, Ontario, Canada K9J 7H5
	2215 Kenmore Ave., Buffalo, New York, USA 14207
	Tel: (705) 743-8990; Fax: (705) 743-8353
	email: customerservice@broadviewpress.com
UK, Europe, Central Asia, Middle East, Africa, India, and Southeast Asia	Eurospan Group, 3 Henrietta St., London WC2E 8LU, United Kingdom Tel: 44 (0) 1767 604972; Fax: 44 (0) 1767 601640 email: eurospan@turpin-distribution.com
Australia and New Zealand	NewSouth Books c/o TL Distribution, 15-23 Helles Ave., Moorebank, NSW, Australia 2170 Tel: (02) 8778 9999; Fax: (02) 8778 9944 email: orders@tldistribution.com.au

www.broadviewpress.com

Broadview Press acknowledges the financial support of the Government of Canada through the Canada Book Fund for our publishing activities.

This book is printed on paper containing 100% postconsumer fibre.

PRINTED IN CANADA

Contributors to *The Broadview Introduction to Literature*

MANAGING EDITORS		Don LePan
		Marjorie Mather
DEVELOPMENTAL AND TEXTUAL EDITOR		Laura Buzzard
EDITORIAL COORDINATORS		Tara Bodie
		Bryanne Miller
CONTRIBUTING EDITORS AND TRANSLATORS		Lisa Chalykoff
		Neta Gordon
		Ian Johnston
		David Swain
CONTRIBUTING WRITERS		Laura Buzzard
		Paul Johnston Byrne
		Tara Bodie

EDITORIAL ASSISTANTS

Tara Bodie	Amanda Mullen
Alicia Christianson	Virginia Philipson
Joel DeShaye	Anja Pujic
Victoria Duncan	Andrew Reszitnyk
Rose Eckert-Jantzie	David Ross
Emily Farrell	Nora Ruddock
Travis Grant	Kate Sinclair
Karim Lalani	Jack Skeffington
Phil Laven	Kaitlyn Till
Kellen Loewen	Morgan Tunzelmann

PRODUCTION COORDINATOR	Tara Lowes
PRODUCTION ASSISTANT	Allison LaSorda
COPY EDITOR	Colleen Franklin
PROOFREADERS	Joe Davies
	Judith Earnshaw
DESIGN AND TYPESETTING	Eileen Eckert
PERMISSIONS COORDINATOR	Merilee Atos
COVER DESIGN	Michel Vrana

Contents

Preface

On hearing that Broadview was planning a new anthology designed to provide an overview of literature at the first-year level, more than a few people have expressed surprise. What could a new anthology have to offer that really is different—that gives something new and valuable to academics and students alike? We hope that you will find your own answers to that question once you have looked through this volume. Certainly our intent has been to offer something that is in many ways different. We have brought fresh eyes to the process of choosing a table of contents; in every genre volume you'll find selections that have not been widely anthologized elsewhere. The very inclusion of literary non-fiction—a form that is increasingly being taken seriously as a literary genre, but that is passed over in most anthologies which purport to offer an overview of literature—is a distinctive feature of our anthology.

Not everything about *The Broadview Introduction to Literature* is entirely new, of course. Many of the selections will, we hope, be familiar to instructors; as to which of the "old chestnuts" continue to work well in a teaching context we have in large part been guided by the advice provided to us by academics at a variety of institutions across Canada. But even where familiar authors and selections are concerned, we think you'll find quite a bit here that is different. We have worked hard to pitch both the author introductions and the explanatory notes at a consistent level throughout—and, in both introductions and notes, to give students more by way of background.

Finally, you'll find fresh material posted on the companion website associated with the anthology. The site <http://sites.broadviewpress.com/BIL/> features additional material on many literary sub-genres and movements; material on writing essays about literature—and on referencing and citation; a much fuller glossary of literary terms than it is possible to include in these pages; and a self-test quiz on the information provided in the introduction to non-fiction. Those wishing to go beyond the choices offered in this volume may assign any one of the more than 300 volumes in the acclaimed Broadview Editions series, and we can arrange to have that volume bundled together with the bound book anthology in a shrink-wrapped package, at little or no additional charge to the student.

Any of the genre volumes of the anthology may also be bundled together in special-price shrink-wrapped packages; whatever genres your course covers, and whatever works you would like to cover within those genres, we will do our best to put together a package that will suit your needs. (Instructors should note that, in addition to the main companion website of materials that may be of interest both to students and to instructors, we have posted instructor-related materials on a separate website.)

I do hope you will like what you see—and I hope as well that you will be in touch with any questions or suggestions; we will always be on the lookout for good ideas as to what we should add to the anthology's companion web-site—and/or for what we should look to include in the next edition of *The Broadview Introduction to Literature*.

[D.L.]

Acknowledgements

The general editors, managing editors, and all of us at Broadview owe a debt of gratitude to the academics who have offered assistance and feedback at various stages of the project:

Rhonda Anderson
Trevor Arkell
Veronica Austen
John Ball
David Bentley
Shashi Bhat
Nicholas Bradley
Jocelyn Coates
Richard Cole
Alison Conway
Heidi J. Tiedemann Darroch
Celeste Daphne Derksen
Lorraine DiCicco
Kerry Doyle
Monique Dumontet
Michelle Faubert
Rebecca Gagan
Jay Gamble
Dana Hansen
Alexander Hart
Linda Harwood
Chandra Hodgson
Kathryn Holland
Ashton Howley
Renee Hulan
Kathleen James-Cavan
Karl Jirgens
Diana Frances Lobb

Kathyrn MacLennan
Shelley Mahoney
Joanna Mansbridge
Mark McDayter
Lindsey McMaster
Susan McNeill-Bindon
Craig Melhoff
Bob Mills
Stephanie Morley
Andrew Murray
Russell Perkin
Allan Pero
Mike Perschon
John Pope
Phyllis Rozendal
Cory Rushton
Laura Schechter
Stephen Schryer
Peter Slade
Marjorie Stone
Daniel Tysdal
Linda Van Netten Blimke
Molly Wallace
David Watt
Nanci White
David Wilson
Dorothy Woodman
Gena Zuroski-Jenkins

The Study of Literature

The Nobel prize-winning physicist Paul Dirac reportedly said, "The aim of science is to make difficult things understandable in a simple way; the aim of poetry is to state simple things in an incomprehensible way." More recently, noted Language poet Charles Bernstein—whose work typically challenges the limits of simple comprehension—published the poem "Thank you for saying thank you," in which he explicitly takes up the issue of how poetry "states" things:

> This is a totally
> accessible poem.
> There is nothing
> in this poem
> that is in any
> way difficult.
> All the words
> are simple &
> to the point.

Though Bernstein's work is undoubtedly meant to register as ironic, both his poem and Dirac's comment draw attention to the idea that literature uses language in a peculiar way, and that one of the most fundamental questions readers of literature must ask themselves is: "How is this said?" Or—with apologies to Dirac—the question might be: "How do the language choices in this text make a seemingly simple thing—for example, a statement about love, or family, or justice, or grief—not incomprehensible, but rather more than just something simple?"

Another way of approaching the question of how literature works is to consider the way this anthology of literature is organized around the idea of genre, with texts chosen and categorized according to the way they fit into the classifications of poetry, short fiction, drama, and literary non-fiction. One way of organizing an introductory anthology of literature is the historical, in which selections are sorted from oldest to most recent, usually grouped together according to what have become acknowledged as distinctive historical periods of literary output. Another is the topical or thematic, in which historically and generically diverse selections are grouped together according to subject matter, so that students may compare differing attitudes toward, for example, gender relations, personal loss, particular historical events, or the process of growing up. The decision by an editor of an anthology—or the instructor of a course—to select one organizing principle over another is not arbitrary, but reflects a choice in terms of teaching students how to approach the reading of literature. In very simple terms, one might regard the three options thus: the historical configuration emphasizes discovering the "what" and "when" of literature—what is the body of written work that has come to be considered "literature" (especially in terms of tracing the outlines of a national literature), and when were examples from this distinguished corpus written? The thematic configuration emphasizes sorting through the "why" of literature—why do writers turn to literature to work through complex ideas, and what can we make of our complex responses to differing, often competing, stances on various topics? The generic configuration, finally, emphasizes the "how" of literature—how is the text put together? What are its working parts? How does an attention to the formal attributes of a literary piece help the reader understand the way it achieves its intellectual and emotional—its more than just simple—effects?

What do literary critics mean when they refer to genre? The word was introduced into the English language sometime in the late eighteenth century, borrowed from the French word *genre*, which meant "kind" or "style" of art, as when the British agricultural reformer Arthur Young refers in his travel narratives to the "genre" of Dutch painting, which he finds wanting in comparison to the work of the Italian masters. We can look back further to the Latin root *genus*, or even the Greek γένος (*génos*), a term which also refers to the idea of a distinct family or clan; thus, the notion of "kind" might helpfully be thought of as a way of thinking about resemblances, relationships, and keys to recognition among the literary genres. Another helpful analogy is the way biologists have taken up the term *genus* as part of the taxonomy of organisms. The term *genus felis*, for example, refers to a particular order of small cats, including such species as the domestic cat (*felis catus*) and the wildcat (*felis silvestris*); both species share common generic attributes, such as a similar size and a preferred diet of small rodents. For biologists and literary critics alike, the concept of genus or genre, respectively, is used to group things together according to a system of shared, identifiable features, with both terms allowing for the idea that larger groupings can be further broken down into even more specific ones (thus we can refer to the various breeds of domestic cats, or the distinctions among the Petrarchan, Shakespearian, and Spenserian sonnets).

Biologists tend to use the word "characteristics" to designate the features of a genus; literary critics, on the other hand, make use of the word "convention," a somewhat more complicated term. Like *characteristics*, the term *conventions* refers to distinguishing elements of a genre, which is why the study of literature requires a thorough understanding of the specialized descriptive vocabulary used to discuss such elements as a text's metre, its narrative point of view, its use of figurative language, etc. The introductions to each section of this anthology will draw attention to this specialized vocabulary, and students will also want to refer to the extensive glossary of literary terms located at the end of the anthology. The idea of convention, though, has additional conceptual importance relating to the way texts are built to be read. While a domestic cat is simply born with retractable claws and a taste for mice, a literary text is constructed, written in a particular way, often with the aim of eliciting a particular response from a reader. The word convention, in this sense, harks back to the legal concept of agreement, so that when writers make use of conventions associated with a genre, they set up a kind of contract with the reader whereby the reader has a sense of what to expect from the text. For example: when the first five minutes of a film include a long shot of the Pentagon, along with a few quickly edited shots of grim-looking military personnel moving quickly through underground hallways, and perhaps a shot of someone in a dark suit yelling into a cellphone, "Operation Silvestris has been aborted!" the audience understands that they are in for some sort of political thriller. They need not know anything about the details of Operation Silvestris to make this interpretive leap, as the presence of a few conventions of the political thriller (the shot of the Pentagon, the phrase "Operation [blank] has been aborted!") are enough to provide the general outline of a contract entered into between film and audience. Likewise, recognizing that a poem has 14 lines and makes use of a rhyming couplet at the end will provide knowledgeable readers of literature with an inkling as to what they should expect, as these readers will be familiar with the structural conventions of the Shakespearean sonnet.

Whereas a legal contract is a fairly straightforward affair—it outlines the terms of agreement for both sides and more or less explicitly refers to the penalties for undermining those terms—the contract between text and reader is multifaceted. One of the most fascinating things about the way writers make use of literary convention is that the terms of agreement are constantly subject to further consideration, thoughtful challenge, or outright derision. Thus, when the speaker of Shakespeare's sonnet 130 refers to his lady's "dun" breasts and "reek[ing]" breath, the point is not to insult his mistress, or even to admire her in a new, more realistic way; rather, the point is to ridicule the way other poets slavishly adhere to the convention that sonnets glorify a woman's beauty, comparing her eyes to the sun and her breath to the smell of roses. This reading is available for the reader who knows that by the time Shakespeare decided to try his hand at the genre, translations and imitations of the Petrarchan sonnet had been circulating at the Elizabethan court for many decades. Like organisms, or even laws, conventions of literature evolve over time as writers seek to rethink the rules of the form they wish to explore. In the prologue to her recent collection *XEclogue*, Lisa Robertson declares, "I needed a genre to gloss my ancestress' complicity with a socially expedient code"; she explains how, in turning to the conventions of the eclogue—a collection of pastoral poems, often satiric—she has found a suitable formal framework for her exploration of the way social insiders and outsiders are marked by class and gender.

Is it somehow problematic to inquire too tenaciously into the working parts of a literary text? Does one risk undermining the emotional force of a poem, the sharp wit of a play, or the exciting plot of an adventure tale if one pays too much attention to seemingly mundane issues of plot structure or metre? To paraphrase a common grievance of the distressed student: by examining the way literature works, are we, somehow, just wrecking it? These questions might, paradoxically, recall Dirac's complaint that literature makes simple things incomprehensible: while we know that literature can manage to communicate difficult notions, making what is mysterious more comprehensible, it is often difficult to articulate or make a viable argument about how it does so. By paying attention to the way a text is built and to the way an author constructs his or her end of the contract, the reader can begin to understand and respond explicitly to the question of how literature produces its particular effects.

Consider the following two textual excerpts:

> Come live with me and be my love,
> And we shall all the pleasures prove.
> (Christopher Marlowe, 1590)

> Boom, boom, boom, let's go back to my room,
> And we can do it all night, and I can make you feel right.
> (Paul Lekakis, 1987)

Based on a quick reading: which excerpt is more appropriate for inclusion in a Valentine's Day card? A poll of employees at Hallmark, not to mention the millions of folks invested in the idea that Valentine's Day is a celebration of romance, would likely make an overwhelming case for the Marlowe excerpt. But why? Answering that question might involve a methodological inquiry into how each excerpt produces a particular response, one which might be broken down into five stages:

Level One: Evaluation—Do I like this text? What is my gut reaction to it?
No doubt, most students of literature have heard an instructor proclaim, with
more or less vitriol, "It doesn't matter if you like the poem/story/play! This
is a literature class, not a book club!" And, while it is true that the evaluative
response does not constitute an adequate final critical response to a text, it's
important to acknowledge one's first reaction. After all, the point of literature
is to produce an effect, sometimes an extreme response. When a text seems
confusing, or hilarious, or provocative, or thrilling, it prompts questions: How
are such effects produced using mere words in particular combinations? Why
would an author want to generate feelings of confusion, hilarity, provocation,
etc.? How am I—the reader—being positioned on the other end of such effects?

Level Two: Interpretation—What is the text about? This is a trickier level
of reading than it might seem. Students sometimes think, mistakenly, that
all literature—and especially poetry—is "open to interpretation," and that
all interpretations are therefore correct. This line of thinking leads to snap,
top-down interpretations, in which the general "mood" of the text is felt
at a gut level (see above), and the ensuing reading of the poem is wrangled
into shape to match that feeling. It is sometimes helpful to think about interpretation as a kind of translation, as in the way those who work at the
United Nations translating talking points from Arabic to Russian are called
"interpreters." Though no translation is flawless, the goal of simultaneous
translation is to get as close as possible to the meaning of the original. Thus,
an interpretation should be thought of as a carefully paraphrased summary
or, for particularly dense works, a line by line explication of the literary text,
both of which may require several rereadings and some meticulous use of
a dictionary. As with reading for evaluation, reading for interpretation can
help generate useful critical questions, such as: How does the way this text
is written affect my attitude toward the subject matter? What is the point of
all the fancy language, which makes this text more or less difficult to inter-
pret? Now that I've figured out what this text is about—at least in terms of
its subject matter—can I begin to determine what sorts of themes are being
tackled?

A note about the distinction between subject matter and **theme**: while
these terms are sometimes used interchangeably, the notion of theme differs
from subject matter in that it implies an idea about or attitude toward the
subject matter. A good rule of thumb to remember is that theme can never be
summed up in just one word (so, there is no such thing as the theme of "Love"
or "Family" or "Women"). Whereas the subject matter of Shakespeare's sonnet
"Shall I compare thee to a summer's day" is admiration or the nature of beauty,

one theme of the poem, arguably, is that the beloved's good qualities are best made apparent in poetry, and that art is superior to nature. Another theme of the poem, arguably, is that the admiration of youth is best accomplished by someone older. Thus, identifying a text's subject matter via interpretation aims to pinpoint a general topic, while the process of contemplating a text's theme is open to elaboration and argumentation.

Level Three: Description—What does the text look like, at least at first glance? Can you give a quick account of its basic formal features? At this level of reading, one starts to think about how a text is built, especially in terms of basic generic features. For example, are we dealing with poetry? Short fiction? Drama? If poetry, can we identify a sub-genre the text fits into—for instance, the sonnet, the ode, or the elegy—and can we begin to assess whether the author is following or challenging conventions associated with that genre? Of course, answering these questions requires prior knowledge of what, for example, a conventional ode is supposed to look like, which is why the student of literature must have a thorough understanding of the specific terminology associated with the discipline. At this level of reading, one might also begin to think about and do some preliminary research on when and where the text was written, so that the issues of literary history and cultural context are broached; likewise, one might begin to think about who is writing the poem, as the matter of the author's societal position might prove a fruitful avenue for further investigation. Thus, a consequent objective at this level of reading is to map the terrain of inquiry, establishing some general facts about the text as building blocks that underpin critical analysis.

Level Four: Analysis—How are particular formal features working, especially as they interact with content? The word analysis comes from the Greek terms ἀνά- (ana-), meaning "throughout," and λύειν (lysis), meaning "to loose." Thus, the procedure for analysis involves taking a text and shaking it apart in order to see more clearly all its particular bits and pieces. This level of reading is akin to putting a text under a microscope. First, one has to identify individual formal features of the text. Then one needs to consider how all the parts fit together. It is at this level that one's knowledge of generic conventions and particular literary techniques—the way figurative language works, the ways in which rhythm and rhyme affect our response to language, the way plotting and point of view can be handled, and so on—is crucial. It may be the case that not everything one notices will find its way into an essay. But the goal at this level of reading should be to notice as much as possible (and it is usually when working at this level that an instructor will be accused of "reading too much into a text," as if that image of a moth beating its wings against a window means nothing more than that the moth is trapped, and that it just happens to have been included in a work). Careful analysis shows that nothing in a text "just happens" to be there. A text is constructed out of special uses of language that beg to be "read into." Reading at this level takes time and a certain amount of expertise so as to tease out how the work is built and begin to understand the connections between form and content.

Level Five: Critical Analysis—How do the formal elements of a literary work connect with what the work has to say to the reader? It is at this level of reading that one begins to make an argument, to develop a thesis. In order to construct a viable thesis, one needs to answer a question, perhaps one of the questions that arose at an earlier level of reading. For example, why does this poem, which seems on the surface to be about love, make use of so many images that have to do with science? What is up with this narrator, who seems to be addressing another character without in any way identifying who he is speaking to? What is significant about the fact that the climax of this play hangs on the matter of whether a guy is willing to sell a portrait? It is at this level of reading, rather than at the level of interpretation, that the literary critic is able to flex his or her creative muscles, as a text poses any number of viable questions and suggests any number of viable arguments. Note, however, that the key word here is "viable." In order to make an argument—in order to convincingly answer a question posed—one must have the textual evidence to make the case, evidence that has been gleaned through careful, meticulous, and thoughtful reading.

Returning now to the two texts, let's see if we can come up with one viable argument as to why Marlowe's text seems more likely to show up in a Valentine's Day card, going through each level of reading to build the foundation—the case—for making that argument.

Level One: Evaluation. At first glance, the Marlowe text just seems more romantic than the Lekakis text: it uses flowery words and has a nice flow to it, while the phrase "do it all night" is kind of blunt and unromantic. On a gut level, one might feel that a Valentine's Day card should avoid such blunt language (although this gut reaction might suggest a first useful research question: why should romance be associated with flowery language rather than blunt expressions?).

Moving on to **Level Two: Interpretation.** Well, the Lekakis text is certainly the more straightforward one when it comes to interpretation, though one has to know that the phrase "do it" refers to having sex as opposed to some other activity (and it is interesting to note that even in the more straightforward text, the author has used a common euphemism). The phrase "Boom boom boom" seems to be untranslatable, which begs the question of why the author used it. Is the phrase still meaningful, even if it's just a series of sounds?

As for the Marlowe text, a careful paraphrase would go something like this: "Move in with me and be my lover, and we can enjoy all kinds of pleasures together." Hmmm—wait a minute: what does the author mean by "pleasures"? Eating good food? Playing card games? Though the word is arguably vague, the references in the first line to moving in together and love make it pretty clear that "pleasures" is another euphemism for having sex (though perhaps a more elegant one than "doing it").

If both texts can be interpreted similarly—both are the words of a would-be lover trying to convince the object of his/her affection to have sex—why does it matter which phrase ends up in a Valentine's Day card? What are the significant differences between each text that cause them to generate distinct gut responses?

Level Three: Description. The Marlowe text, at least this piece of it, is a **couplet**, written in iambic **tetrameter** (or eight syllables in each line that follow the rhythmic pattern of unstressed/stressed). The language is flowery, or, to use a slightly more technical phrase, the **diction** is elevated, which means that this is not the way people normally talk in everyday life. In fact, there seems to have been a lot of attention paid to making the words sound pleasing to the ear, through patterns of rhythm and rhyme, and also through patterns of alliteration in the consonants (of the soft "l" sound in the first line, and then of powerful plosives at the end of the second).

The Lekakis text also makes use of rhyme, but in a different way: each line includes an **internal rhyme**, so that "boom" rhymes with "room" and "night" rhymes with "right." The rhythmic pattern is harder to make sense of, as there are a different number of syllables in each line and a lot of short, sharp words that undermine a sing-song effect. The sound effects of the text are comparatively harsher than in the Marlowe text, with many "b" and "k" and "t" sounds.

The Marlowe text was written in the 1590s, while the Lekakis text is a popular dance song from the 1980s; it might be interesting to follow up on the distinct cultural contexts out of which each work emerges. It might also be interesting to examine how each text thematizes the subject of having sex: whereas the Marlowe text seems to promote the attitude that the "pleasures" of sex should be tried out (to "prove" in sixteenth-century English meant to test or to try out) within the context of "living with" someone, or that love and sex go hand-in-hand, the Lekakis text seems to suggest that even sex on one "night" in someone's "room" can make one feel "right." Or, good sex has nothing at all to do with love.

Because these texts are so short and are fairly simple, much of the work of **Level Four: Analysis** has already been touched on. A closer inspection of the use of rhyme and **alliteration** in the Marlowe text demonstrates the way the poem insists on the idea that love can be "proved" by sex, while the internal rhyming of the words "me," "be," and "we" further indicates a strong emphasis on how the joining of two people represents a significant change. The use of elevated diction is consistent, suggesting that discussions of love and sex are worthy of serious consideration.

As for the Lekakis text, a major point to analyze is the phrase "boom boom boom." Is this **onomatopoeia**? If so, what "sense" is the sound trying to express? The sound of sex? If so, what kind of sex are we talking about here? Or is it the sound of something else, perhaps dancing (as is suggested by the cultural context of which the text emerges)? Maybe the phrase is simply meant to express excitement? What do we make of the plain speech the text employs? Does the use of such diction debase notions of sex, or is it simply more candid about the way sex and love might be separated?

As you can see, the level of **Critical Analysis**, or argument, is quickly and organically developing. If the research question one decides on is, What is interesting about the distinct way each text thematizes the relationship between love and sex?, a viable argument, based on evidence gleaned from close reading, might be: "Whereas Marlowe's text suggests that the pleasures of sex are best discovered within the context of a stable, long-term relationship, the text by Lekakis asserts that sex can be enjoyed in and of itself, undermining the importance of the long-term relationship." One might take this argument further. Why is what you have noted significant or particularly interesting? A possible answer to that question—and an even more sophisticated thesis—might be: "Thus, while the Lekakis text is, on the surface, less romantic, its attitude toward sex is much less confining than the attitude presented in Marlowe's text." Or, one might pursue an entirely different argument: "Whereas Marlowe's text indicates that sex is to be enjoyed mutually by two people, the Lekakis text implies that sex is something one 'does' to another person. Further, it implies that sex is a fairly meaningless and potentially aggressive activity."

The above description of the steps taken toward critical analysis shows how students of literature are meant to approach the works they read. What the description does not convey is why one would bother to make the effort at all, or why the process of critical literary analysis is thought to be a meaningful activity. In order to answer that question, it is helpful to consider how the discipline of literary studies came to be considered a worthwhile course of study for university and college students.

The history of literary studies is both very old and, in terms of the study of English literature, very fresh. In the fifth century, Martianus Capella wrote the allegory *De nuptiis Philologiae et Mercurii* ("The Marriage of Philology and Mercury"), in which he described the seven pillars of learning: grammar, dialectic, rhetoric, geometry, arithmetic, astronomy, and musical harmony. Collectively, such subjects came to be referred to as the liberal arts; as such, they were taken up by many of the high medieval universities as constituting the core curriculum. During the Early Modern period, the study of the so-called *trivium* (grammar, dialectic, rhetoric) was transformed to include the critical analysis of classical texts, i.e., the study of literature. As universities throughout Europe, and later in North America, proliferated and flourished between the sixteenth and nineteenth centuries, the focus remained on classical texts. As Gerald Graff explains, "In theory, the study of Greek and Latin was supposed to inspire the student with the nobility of his cultural heritage." (Somewhat paradoxically, classical texts were studied primarily in terms of their language use as opposed to their literary quality, perhaps because no one read or spoke Greek or Latin outside the classroom.) Until the late nineteenth century, the university system did not consider literary works written in English (or French or German or Italian) to be worthy of rigorous study, but only of *appreciation*. As Terry Eagleton notes in *Literary Theory: An Introduction*, the reading of works of English Literature was thought best left to working-class men, who might attend book clubs or public lectures, and to women; it was "a convenient sort of non-subject to palm off on the ladies, who were in any case excluded from science and the professions." It was only in the early twentieth century—hundreds of years after the founding of the great European universities—that literature came to be taken seriously as a university or college subject.

Over the past century and more, the discipline of literary studies has undergone a number of shifts. In the very early twentieth century, literature was studied largely for the way in which it embodied cultural tradition; one would learn something about being American or British by reading so-called great works of literature. (As British subjects, Canadians were also taught what it was to be a part of the British tradition.) By mid-century the focus had shifted to the aesthetic properties of the work itself. This fresh approach was known as Formalism and/or the New Criticism. Its proponents advocated paying close attention to literary form—in some cases, for an almost scientific approach to close reading. They tended to de-emphasize authorial biography and literary history. The influence of this approach continues to be felt in university and college classrooms (giving rise to such things as, for example, courses organized around the concept of literary genre). But it is important to keep in mind here that the emphasis on form—on generic conventions, on literary terminology, on the aesthetic as opposed to the cultural, philosophical, or moral qualities of literature—is not the only way to approach the study of literature, but was, rather, institutionalized as the best, most scholarly way. The work of close reading and producing literary criticism is not in any way "natural," but is how the study of literature has been "disciplined"; thus the student in a literature classroom should not feel discouraged if the initial steps of learning what it is he or she is supposed to be doing are challenging or seem strange.

The most recent important shift to have occurred in the "disciplining" of literary studies was the rise in the 1960s and 1970s of what became known as "literary theory." There is not room enough here to adequately elucidate the range of theories that have been introduced into literary studies, but a crude comparison between how emerging methods were set in opposition to New Criticism (which is itself a type of literary theory) may be useful. John Crowe Ransom's *The World's Body*—a sort of manifesto for New Criticism—argues that the work of the literary critic must strenuously avoid, among other things, "Any other special studies which deal with some abstract or prose content taken out of the work ... [such as] Chaucer's command of medieval sciences ... [or] Shakespeare's understanding of the law." In other words, the New Critic should focus solely on the text itself. In contrast, those today who make use of such theoretical frameworks as New Historicism, Gender Studies, or Postcolonial Studies will strenuously *embrace* all manner of "special studies" in order to consider how the text interacts with context. As Graff puts it, "Theory is what is generated when some aspect of literature, its nature, its history, its place in society, its conditions for production and reception, its meaning in general ... ceases to be a given and becomes a question to be argued." What this means for the student of literature trying to work out what to do with a text is that the question "Why is what I have noticed in the text significant?" can be approached from an almost limitless set of knowledge contexts. How might a particular poem illuminate historical notions of class divisions? How might a particular play tell us something about how technological advances have changed the way humans think about identity? And, though it might seem that the focus on form that so defines the New Critical approach becomes irrelevant once Literary Theory arrives on the disciplinary scene, the fact is that most field practitioners (i.e., writers of literary criticism) still depend heavily on the tools of close reading; formal analysis becomes the foundation on which a more theoretical analysis is built.

Thus, we might consider a sixth level of reading: advanced critical analysis. At this level the stakes are raised as arguments about why a text's formal construction is meaningful are set within a larger conceptual framework. The work of advanced critical analysis requires that the literary critic think about and research whatever conceptual framework is being pursued. For example, after noticing that the Marlowe text and the Lekakis text are written about 400 years apart, one might further research cultural attitudes toward sex in the two time periods to come up with another, even more sophisticated, layer of argumentation, one which would not only provide insight into two literary texts, but show how the comparative analysis of such texts tells us something about how viewpoints on sex have shifted. Or, after noticing that both texts are written by male authors, one might further research and consider what they reveal about masculine approaches to sex and seduction. Or, after discovering that Marlowe's poem follows the conventions of **pastoral** poetry, or that "Boom boom boom (let's go back to my room)" became popular within the LGBT community, one might contemplate and develop an argument about the implications of the way sex is idealized and/or becomes part of a complex cultural fantasy. Or, after discovering that Marlowe presented homoerotic material frequently in his other writing (in his poem "Hero and Leander," for example, he writes of one of the male protagonists that "in his looks were all that men desire"), one might inquire into the ways in which the author's or narrator's sexual orientation may or may not be relevant to a discussion of a love poem. To put it bluntly (and anachronistically), does it matter if Marlowe was gay?

Because the reading of literature entails a painstaking, thoughtful interaction with some of the most multifaceted, evocative, and provocative uses of language humans have produced, thinking about such work critically may tell us something about what it means to be human.

[N.G.]

Literary Non-Fiction

L iterary non-fiction is a diverse genre with a long history—yet its nature is hard to pin down. A work of literary non-fiction is nowadays almost always written in prose, but it may be an essay, a memoir, a piece of journalism. It may be written for any one of a wide range of purposes. It may be as short as a page or two, or it may be of book length.

No work that calls itself "non-fiction" can be the product of pure invention—if you make up the story, you are writing fiction. Yet the line that separates fiction from non-fiction may sometimes be hard to determine. Many authors of literary non-fiction consider it a legitimate practice to shape the presentation of events or characters in an essay or a memoir in ways that deviate from the specifics of what actually happened. George Orwell, one of the most highly acclaimed writers of literary non-fiction of the twentieth century, is known to have done this frequently. So too, in the preface to one of the most influential works of literary non-fiction of the new century, *Dreams of My Father*, does Barack Obama candidly acknowledge that at least part of what he has written is, in some sense, fiction:

> Although much of this book is based on contemporaneous journals or the oral histories of my family, the dialogue is necessarily an approximation of what was actually said or relayed to me. For the sake of compression, some of the characters that appear are composites of people I've known, and some events appear out of precise chronology.

In other words, the writer has felt at liberty to sift and shape the material to give a personal view of what seems to him to be, in his words, "some granite slab of truth." Obama goes on to acknowledge the difficulty in naming this sort of writing: "Whatever the label that attaches to this book—autobiography, memoir, family history, or something else—what I've tried to do is write an honest account of a particular province of my life." Critics have reached different conclusions as to whether or not the picture that emerges does in fact present "some granite slab of truth"; they disagree as to the degree to which such a work should be thought of as non-fiction. But virtually all have agreed—in much the same way as they have agreed about acclaimed non-fiction works by Orwell, such as "Shooting an Elephant," or *Down and Out in Paris and London*—that it should be thought of as literature.

Literary Non-Fiction and Academic Non-Fiction

The form that literary non-fiction most frequently takes is that of the essay. But an *essay* in this sense is something very different from the kind of essay that university students are asked to read (and, usually, to write) when they take courses in academic subjects. For the most part, students are taught that an academic essay should be distanced and impersonal. It should be structured according to established conventions of its academic discipline. And according to these conventions, the academic essay should strive for objectivity; subjective reflections that cannot be supported with evidence have little place in this kind of writing. The task of the essay writer is not to sway the reader through description or narration or emotional appeal of any sort, but rather to analyze evidence in support of an argument. Whether that argument is made inductively or deductively, an academic essay should display careful reasoning according to logical principles. It should also cite references to support its argument—and to make it easier for other students and scholars to verify the evidence and engage with the argument in a scholarly manner.

The sort of essay that constitutes a work of literary non-fiction is none of these things. Though it may sometimes marshal evidence in support of a reasoned argument, it may also employ narration and description and emotional appeal. It may be loosely structured. It is more likely to be personal in tone. And it will normally not include any cited sources.[1] Whereas the academic essay is generally addressed to an audience within a particular scholarly academic discipline, literary non-fiction is typically addressed to a broad audience. It aims to interest and entice readers and to give them pleasure, in the way that literature gives pleasure—through the use of well-crafted images, figurative language, and symbols, by ordering events to create suspense, and by creating interesting non-fictional "characters" to engage us.

Such pleasure is not contingent on the writer's topic being pleasurable. Just as a novel about horrific events can be, *as literature*, enjoyable as well as interesting to read, so too a piece of literary non-fiction about horrific events can be, *as literature*, enjoyable. Conveying in memorable and affecting ways the "unspeakable" is an important function of literature. Philip Gourevitch's piece in this volume, reflecting on the nature of genocide and on having seen

---

1   An essay such as David Foster Wallace's "Consider the Lobster" is in this respect less of an exception than it might seem. For the most part it employs notes not to cite sources but to provide tangential reflections—reflections that are surely of interest but that might act as a distraction if included in the body of the essay.

the aftermath of a massacre, falls squarely into this category. But if, as a general question, we ask what sorts of topics literary non-fiction addresses, there is no simple answer. The writer may work through any one of a wide range of structures in trying to mediate a reader's understanding of an endless variety of topics. Examples in this volume include an exploration of a father's life (Miriam Toews's memoir); an argument about the appeal of wrestling (Roland Barthes); a discussion of a lobster festival—and of the practice of boiling lobsters alive (David Foster Wallace); reflections tinged with double-edged humour on having a mixed cultural heritage (Drew Hayden Taylor); and an evocation of the thrill of travelling to a new country (Karen Connelly). In all literary non-fiction, though, style and structure are determined not by the conventions of an academic discipline, but by literary values—and by the writer's personality.

History of the Genre

Given that literary non-fiction has only recently begun to receive considerable attention as a distinct literary genre, one might easily imagine that writing of this sort would be a relatively recent phenomenon. In fact, its roots go almost as far back as do those of poetry and drama. Like them, the genre of literary non-fiction has strong roots in the classical cultures of ancient Greece and Rome. The ancients referred to the process of communication as *rhetoric*. Broadly defined, rhetoric may be said to be involved in almost anything to do with the study of cultural messages, with any communication that attempts to persuade, with almost every human effort to express thoughts coherently so as to communicate them to others. In practice, the Greeks and Romans defined rhetoric much more narrowly. Classical rhetoric was an art whose precepts were designed to help orators (*rhetors*) organize and deliver their arguments in a methodical, articulate, and persuasive way. That may sound a long way from the literary non-fiction of today—may sound, indeed, of more relevance to the roots of the modern academic essay than to those of literary non-fiction. And there can be no question of the relevance of classical rhetoric to the history of academic argument. But historians suggest that the modern essay as a work of literary non-fiction may also be found in embryonic form in the works of some classical writers—not least of all in a work now almost two thousand years old, the *Moral Letters* of the Roman Stoic philosopher Lucius Annaeus Seneca (usually known simply as Seneca).

Though the 124 pieces that make up the *Moral Letters* are written as letters to the then-governor of Sicily, Lucilius—each one begins "Seneca greets his Lucilius"—in every other respect the epistles far more closely resemble what we now call literary non-fiction than they do modern-day personal letters. They are personal in tone, to be sure, but they include little or nothing relating to the particulars of the personal relationship between Seneca and Lucilius. They seem rather to address a general audience. As is the case with the piece on masters and slaves included here, Seneca's epistles often discuss broad topics, and they often put forth a persuasive argument. They often employ narration (as Seneca does in recounting his little story about Callistus) and description (as when he gives us a picture of the dining table or describes the master whose greed has filled his distended belly). They often appeal to the senses and to the emotions at least as much as to reason. Each piece focuses on a particular topic—but the topics tend to be broad and range widely, from drunkenness to scientific invention, to how a love of sports can become excessive, to the issue of equality between men and women. Seneca is thought of today primarily as a philosopher, but in the *Moral Letters* his writing is far closer to that of today's writer of literary essays than it is to the writing of most contemporary philosophers.

In the post-medieval era the literary essay is generally said to have begun with the sixteenth-century French writer Michel de Montaigne, known in his day as the "French Seneca." Like Seneca, Montaigne wrote short pieces on a wide variety of broad topics ranging from marriage to study, education, and various aspects of current affairs. But Montaigne's pieces tend to be both more closely reasoned than those of Seneca, and looser in structure. More often than not they explore an idea rather than set out an argument in favour of a predetermined position. Montaigne saw writing of this sort less as a means of persuading the reader to accept a certain conclusion than as a means of trying to grope one's way toward understanding. Hence the name he gave to these short pieces—*essais*, or, in English, *attempts* or *tries*. (The connection is a direct one; among its definitions of *essay* the *Oxford English Dictionary* offers the following: "the action or process of trying or testing.") And always, while attempting to understand some aspect of an idea or of the world, Montaigne was attempting to understand himself—reflecting on his own thoughts, impulses, and desires. In the preface to the *Essais* Montaigne famously declares, "lecteur, je suis moi-même la matière de mon livre" ("reader, I am myself the subject of my book"). In all these respects—the looseness of structure, the vision of writing as a means of groping toward understanding, the tendency to use the essay to explore the outside world and the self simultaneously—Montaigne's writing continues to exert an influence on literary non-fiction.

The history of the literary essay in English is extraordinarily varied. It is often said to begin in early seventeenth-century England with the very Montaigne-like essays of Francis Bacon. With the eighteenth century came the pointed political and literary essays of Samuel Johnson and Jonathan Swift, and the beginnings of literary journalism. The nineteenth century brought the cultural criticism of Charles Dickens, Matthew Arnold, and George Eliot in Britain, and the personal-philosophic essays of Henry David Thoreau and Ralph Waldo Emerson in the United States. In the twentieth century the range of literary non-fiction became broader still, from Virginia Woolf's essays on gender and society and George Orwell's explorations of politics and culture, to the fresh approaches to form and the tremendous variety of subject matter that characterize the literary non-fiction of late twentieth- and early twenty-first-century writers from every corner of the globe. Across this diversity, though, direct links to the traditions of Montaigne and Seneca remain—in tone, style, structure, and rhetorical strategies.

Style and Structure, Argument, and Rhetoric

Let's return to our comparison of how arguments are presented in the modern academic essay versus literary non-fiction. As we have said, reason and logic are central to what the writer of the academic essay strives for, and the logic of the argument is made overt through such conventions as thesis statements and topic sentences. Anything that might impede an impersonal and objective presentation of a reasoned argument is often said to be inappropriate in an academic essay. Rhetorical flourishes are kept to a minimum. The structure in which an argument is presented tends to be standardized. The pronoun "I" is often said to have no place here, and the same is said of personal details or reflections. Style and structure, in short, are conventionalized in order for the writer to be as unobtrusive as possible—and in order to allow reasoned argument to shine through.

In literary non-fiction, on the other hand, a range of structures is available to the writer, and the adoption of a personal tone and a unique style are often very much a part of the presentation of the "argument." Why is the word "argument" put in quotation marks here? To make clear that, in the context of literary non-fiction, *argument* is not to be taken in the same sense as it is with most academic non-fiction. The argument of a piece of literary non-fiction is the line along which ideas are connected; it may be much looser and less overt than the argument of the typical academic paper of today, and its logic may be implicit, to be sought out by the reader.

Whether we are looking at non-literary academic arguments or those of literary non-fiction, the vocabulary of classical rhetoric remains highly useful when it comes to naming the elements of argument. According to one of the most influential classical rhetorical manuals, *Rhetorica ad Herennium* (which dates from the first century BCE), rhetoric has five canons or general, fundamental principles: invention, arrangement, style, memory, and delivery. As may readily be inferred from the last two items on that list, the expectation was that rhetorical arguments would be delivered orally through a speech (by a *rhetor*) rather than in writing. But the strength and originality of the ideas (invention), the way in which they are arranged, and the style with which they are presented are concepts that remain relevant to non-fiction writing of all sorts.

The *Rhetorica ad Herennium* also sets out guidelines for the layout of an argument (in classical terminology, its *disposition*), specifying that it should include the following elements:

- exordium (introduces the argument)

- narration (states the issue; may supply background or explore the history of the issue)

- division (separates and lists the parts under discussion)

- confirmation (elaborates and supports the *rhetor*'s position)

- confutation (refutes opposing arguments)

- peroration (conclusion)

We may observe these elements in Seneca's writing—how he separates the arts under discussion, how he anticipates (and refutes) the arguments of his opponents. Aside perhaps from *exordium* and *peroration*, though, it may well be thought that such concepts are of limited use in analyzing the contemporary literary essay. But from time to time they may indeed be useful in discussing literary non-fiction. We may see traces of the classical rhetorical strategies of narration and division, for example, in the way in which David Foster Wallace fills in some of the history of lobster eating and guides the reader through the parts of his argument.

Ancient guides to rhetoric also often considered arguments as belonging to one of three types: deliberative (concerned with the future), judicial (sometimes referred to as forensic; concerned with the past), and epideictic (celebratory arguments). These classifications too may sometimes be helpful in discussions of literary non-fiction. When Mark Twain addresses an imaginary audience in "Advice to Youth," he creates an epideictic argument. Roland Barthes, as he explores "The World of Wrestling," makes a judicial or forensic argument (as do several of the other selections). Deliberative arguments in anything close to a pure form, however, are rarely found in literary non-fiction; they occur far more frequently in politicians' speeches, in the arguments of newspaper and television commentators—or in the world of advertising.

Perhaps of greater relevance to today's literary non-fiction are the three categories of appeal that are set out in classical rhetoric (from the early Greek philosopher Aristotle on down): *logos*, *pathos*, and *ethos*. All three are widely and usefully employed in many discussions of literary writing today.

Logos is often translated as *logic*, and to a large extent appeals based on *logos* may indeed be appeals that are logical in nature. But in the world of rhetoric such appeals are not always made according to the principles of inductive or deductive logic that apply to most academic essays. The meaning of *logos* in the ancient world was multi-faceted; it could mean *reason* or *logic*, but it could also simply mean *word*; in the context of literary non-fiction, an appeal based on *logos* may perhaps best be understood as an appeal based on the ideas that the words hold. The rational arguments that Seneca makes—appealing to the principle of fairness and citing the benefits of treating one's slaves or servants well—represent appeals to *logos*. Much the same can be said of Barthes's arguments about the moral content of wrestling. These are arguments that in large part make appeals to *logos* based on traditional principles of logical reasoning. But Miriam Toews also makes an appeal to *logos* when she recounts the history in the Mennonite church of shunning those "out of faith"—a category that included those suffering from depression or despair—and then writes that she "can't help thinking" that this history of shunning had "just a little to do with" the ways in which her father tried to deal with his depression. Toews's line of reasoning cannot be said to follow the same sorts of logical steps that the arguments of Barthes or Seneca do—and she makes no claims to have reached an airtight conclusion. Yet her appeal to *logos* may be more powerful than that of any of the other pieces included here. Rather than establishing the tenets of and the conclusion to an argument, her appeal to *logos* suggests connections. And rather than demonstrating irrefutably that those connections exist, she persuades us that they are likely to have played a real part in what happened to her father. Giving readers freedom in this way to discern an argument's logic by forging connections for themselves is one important way in which the genre of literary non-fiction may exert powerful effects.

The word *pathos* is sometimes thought to hold pejorative connotations, describing an appeal to the emotions that is too contrived, blatant, or superficial. Appeals to the emotions may surely be all of those things. But they need not be any of them and certainly the term *pathos*, properly used, carries much the same meaning today as it did for the ancients, referring to any appeal to the emotions. Such appeals have a legitimate place in most forms of argumentation, given that our responses to experiences inevitably involve both heart and head; indeed, many would argue that the direction our reason takes is always informed at some level by our initial, emotional responses. Such appeals may take many forms. When you read Gourevitch's "We Wish to Inform You That

Tomorrow We Will Be Killed with Our Families" or Orwell's "Shooting an Elephant," you will likely be moved by the full sweep of the experience the writer is recounting. Toews's "A Father's Faith" is another example of a piece in which an appeal to *pathos* arguably runs throughout the essay. But appeals to *pathos* may be embedded even in very brief descriptions that have strong emotive content. Seneca's sentence describing the master and his distended belly (evoking in the reader the emotion of disgust at his display of greed) is a case in point.

For Aristotle and other ancient Greek authorities, an appeal to *ethos* was one based on the character of the person presenting the argument, whether that might have to do with the speaker's position of authority, his or her perceived honesty, or other ethical virtues. In modern usage, *ethos* is still used to refer to the character of the person putting forward an argument, but there may be more factors that come into play today in determining this character. The idea of authority is a case in point. Though our society's more populist impulses may make us less inclined to judge the merits of a given argument on the basis of the writer's credentials, reputation still influences the willingness many of us have to extend faith to authors. When Roland Barthes begins "The World of Wrestling" with the bold, seemingly contradictory claim that "The virtue of all-in wrestling is that it is a spectacle of excess," we are in part inclined to give the thought credence, or extend some faith that it will in fact become sensible, because it comes from such an esteemed thinker. Similarly, the idea of virtue today is somewhat more complicated: it is now quite widely accepted that we do not in fact have reliable information as to the virtues—or lack thereof—of the writer of an essay. Yet we can gain a sense of whether a writer seems virtuous or not from any number of tiny cues—in the compassion we may sense in an author's treatment of a subject, or, by contrast, in his or her failure to judge others generously. What this means is that, generally speaking, appeals to *ethos* may be considered to rest on a wider range of characteristics today, for instance on our knowledge of a given speaker and the way in which speakers present themselves, or on the overall personality that we sense behind a particular piece of writing.

Unlike the structural elements of logical arguments (whether as set out according to the principles of classical rhetoric, or according to those of modern manuals for academic essay writing), the sorts of appeals that literary non-fiction makes (to *logos*, *pathos*, and *ethos*) are unlikely ever to follow one upon the other in a predictable order. Appeals to logic may alternate with appeals to emotion, just as narrative and descriptive and argumentative passages may be interspersed one with another. Such alternation is a continual feature of a number of the pieces of literary non-fiction included here, including those by Gourevitch, Toews, and Foster Wallace. Arguments that are almost academic in their tone may alternate with paragraphs in which appeals to *ethos* and *pathos* come to the fore. There may be sudden turns; surprise is a strategy that we tend to associate with narrative fiction but also one that may feature prominently in literary non-fiction. Surprise may be said, for example, to be part of the structure of the Gourevitch piece, as it surely is of Toews's.

It may be appropriate to end this introduction to literary non-fiction with one more glance in the direction of the two points of comparison we've used throughout: the principles of classical rhetoric and those of modern academic essay writing. Both those sets of principles are prescriptive: Aristotle and other ancient classical authorities were endeavouring to explain to their readers how arguments should be structured; the precepts of classical rhetoric were designed to help orators organize and deliver their speeches in a methodical, articulate way. Similarly, modern manuals of essay writing aim to explain to students how such essays should be written; they are designed to help students follow the established conventions of an academic discipline. It is more difficult—perhaps impossible—to provide a blueprint for how to write literary non-fiction—and certainly this introduction makes no attempt to do so. It aims to be descriptive rather than prescriptive—to give some sense of the characteristics of the genre of literary non-fiction, and some sense as well of the degree to which an understanding of rhetorical principles may foster a broader understanding of the lines of argument that contemporary writers of literary non-fiction put forward, and the means of expression they employ in doing so. The selections here do not aim to trace the historical development of the genre. They are intended rather to be representative of the genre as it has developed—to provide some sense, however limited, of its diversity and versatility.

—P.L.

‍ucius Annaeus Seneca

c. 4 BCE–65 CE

A philosopher, orator, and tragedian who produced works of lasting significance in each genre he attempted, Lucius Annaeus Seneca was among Imperial Rome's most versatile and admired men of letters. The dark vision and violent emotion of his tragedies, which resound with rhetorically elaborate speeches voiced by characters at extremes of distress, greatly influenced many Tudor and Jacobean dramatists, including Shakespeare. The impact of his prose works, in which he often adopts the persona of a moral or spiritual adviser who addresses the reader in an engagingly frank and personal style, was similarly far-reaching, providing writers such as Montaigne with a model for the introspective essay.

In addition to his literary accomplishments, Seneca was also a statesman. Banished in the wake of allegations of adultery, he was recalled from exile to be a teacher to the young Nero; when Nero became emperor, Seneca rose to political prominence as a senior advisor to his former pupil. For almost a decade, Seneca occupied the very centre of power in Rome, but his influence began to ebb as the emperor became increasingly erratic and extravagant. With his position growing more tenuous, Seneca eventually withdrew to private life, but Nero nevertheless accused him of involvement in a conspiracy and ordered him to commit suicide.

Before Nero's cruel ultimatum, which he obeyed with composure in a scene famously recorded by Tacitus, Seneca wrote his masterpiece, the *Moral Letters to Lucilius* (c. 65 CE). A series of 124 essays presented as a correspondence addressed to Lucilius Iunior, the governor of Sicily, the *Letters* represent a major contribution to Stoic philosophy. Like many later Stoics, Seneca was especially interested in ethics, and the *Letters* describe a course of moral therapy intended to improve the reader's character by offering guidance in how to subdue emotion through reason and so maintain self-possession in the face of adversity.

Epistle 47[1] from *Moral Letters to Lucilius*

I was pleased to learn from those who come from you that you live on familiar terms with your slaves. That is appropriate for a man of your intelligence and education. "They are slaves," people say. No—they are people. "They are *slaves*." No—they are attendant comrades. "But slaves is what they are." No—

---

1   *Epistle 47* Translation prepared for this anthology by Ian Johnston, Vancouver Island University.

they are unassuming friends. "They are slaves." No—they are *fellow*-slaves, if *anaphora* you recognize that Fortune values both me and them quite equally.

And so I laugh at those who think it is demeaning to dine with one of their own slaves. Why would they think this, unless the reason is that our proudest customs require the master at his dinner to have a crowd of slaves standing around him? He eats more than he can hold and, in his enormous greed, stuffs his swollen belly, which now no longer functions as a stomach. So with a greater effort than it took to gorge himself he vomits up the entire meal. Meanwhile, the unhappy slaves are not permitted to move their lips, not even to speak. The rod suppresses every murmur. Even a random noise— a cough, a sneeze, a hiccup—earns them the whip. The punishment for any word that interrupts the silence is extremely harsh. All night long, the slaves stand there, mute and hungry.

As a result, those who are not permitted to speak in the presence of their master, talk about him. However, when slaves whose mouths were not stitched shut used to talk not only in the presence of their masters but also with them, they were prepared to stretch their necks out for their master's sake, to let any imminent threat to him fall on their heads. They would talk during the feast, but during torture they were silent. Later, thanks to this arrogance of masters the proverb spread, "To have as many enemies as one has slaves." When we acquire slaves, they are not enemies, but we make them our foes.

At the moment I will overlook other cruel and inhuman ways we treat our *prolepsis* slaves, for we abuse them as if they were not even human beings, but beasts of burden. While we recline at ease to dine, one slave wipes up the vomit, another, crouching underneath the table, collects the leavings of the drunken guests. Another carves the expensive birds. With a practiced hand his sure strokes cut around the breast and rump, and he serves the portions, unhappy man who lives for this one task of carving plump fowl skillfully—unless the person who for pleasure's sake instructs this skill is even more unhappy than the one who learns it from necessity. Still another slave, who serves the wine and wears a woman's fancy clothes, struggles against his age, for he cannot escape being dragged back to his boyish years. By now he has a soldier's look, but his hair is scraped away or plucked out by the root to keep him beardless, and he must stay awake all night, dividing his time between his master's drunkenness and lust: in the bedroom he is a man, and at the feast a boy. Another one, whose job is to evaluate the guests, keeps standing there in misery to watch for those whose fawning flattery and intemperance in what they eat or what they say will invite them back tomorrow. Think of the ones who must prepare the feast, those with subtle expertise about their master's palate, who know the things whose taste excites it, whose appearance pleases him, whose novelty can rouse him from his nausea, as well as which foods will now disgust him if he gets too much and which will stimulate his appetite that day. With these slaves the master does not deign to eat. He believes that coming to the same table with his own slave diminishes his majesty. God forbid!

How many masters is he acquiring with slaves like these! I have observed Callistus'[1] master—the one who stuck a bill of sale on him and took him to the market with the useless slaves—standing before Callistus' door and kept outside while others entered. Callistus was included in the first job lot of slaves on which the auctioneer warms up his voice, and now the slave has paid his master back by rejecting him, in turn, and judging him unworthy to come in his house. The master sold Callistus, but how much has Callistus made his master pay!

You would do well to recognize that the man you call your slave sprang from the same seeds as you, enjoys the same sky, breathes, lives, and dies just as you do! You can look on him as a free born man, as much as he can see you as a slave. In that disaster caused by Marius,[2] many men of very splendid birth, preparing for a senatorial rank by military service, were sunk by Fortune, who made one of them a shepherd and another the custodian of a cottage. Now condemn the man whose change in fortune you may share while you condemn him.

I have no wish to involve myself in a huge issue and to explore the way we treat our slaves, towards whom we are excessively proud, cruel, and abusive. But the main thrust of my advice is this: live with your inferiors just as you would wish your superior to live with you. Whenever it crosses your mind how much you can do quite lawfully to a slave of yours, think about how much your master can legally inflict on you.

"But I," you may well say, "don't have a master." You are still young. Perhaps you will have one. Do you not know how old Hecuba was when she became a slave—or Croesus, or Darius' mother, or Plato, or Diogenes?[3]

Live with your slave calmly, even as a friend. Let him enter your conversations, your deliberations, and your social intercourse. At this point the whole crowd of those spoiled with luxury will complain to me: "Nothing would be

---

1   *Callistus* Gaius Julius Callistus (first century CE), a freed Roman slave who rose to political prominence.

2   *Marius* Gaius Marius (157–86 BCE) was a Roman general and politician. Near the end of his life his achievement of political authority brought about a brief period of murderous attacks against many prominent Romans.

3   *Hecuba* Wife of Priam, king of Troy. She became a slave after the city fell; *Croesus* Fabulously rich and powerful king of Lydia in the sixth century BCE. He was defeated and enslaved by the Persians; *Darius* Persian emperor (fourth century BCE) conquered by Alexander the Great; *Plato, or Diogenes* The Greek philosophers Plato (c. 427–c. 347 BCE) and Diogenes (fourth century BCE) also were captured and briefly enslaved.

more degrading than this, nothing more repulsive." These are the same people I will discover kissing the hand of other people's slaves.

Surely you recognize the fact that our ancestors removed everything invidious from the masters and everything insulting from the slaves? They called the master *father of the family*, and the slaves *members of the household*, a practice which still continues in the mimes.[1] They set up a festival day when masters ate with their slaves, but that was not the only time this happened. They assigned slaves honours in the house, permitted them to render judgment, and considered the house a miniature commonwealth.

"What then? Shall I bring all my slaves to my own table?" No. No more than you would bring all free men there. You are wrong if you think I would bar certain men who do more menial work—like, say, that herdsman or that slave who tends the mules. I will not judge them by the work they do, but by their characters. Each person gives himself his character; chance gives him his work. Let some slaves dine with you because they are worthy men, and dine with some to make them worthy. For if debased associations have made them servile, then the society of distinguished men will shake that off.

My dear Lucilius, you should not look for a friend only in the forum or the senate house. If you pay attention carefully, you will find one at home. Often without a skilled artist, good material is wasted. Try and you will find that out. Just as someone who is going to purchase a horse is a fool if he inspects the saddle and the bridle but not the animal itself, so that person is extremely stupid who evaluates a man either by his clothes or by his social condition (which, like our robes, is merely a cover).

"He is a slave." But perhaps his spirit is free. "He is slave." Will that make him culpable? Show me who is not a slave. One man is a slave to lust, another to avarice, another to ambition, and all are slaves to fear. I will show you an ex-consul enslaved to a little old woman, a rich man enslaved to a young serving maid. I will point out young men of the highest rank who are slaves of pantomimes! No slavery is more repulsive than voluntary servitude.

And so those fastidious types should not prevent you from acting affably with your slaves rather than proudly superior. To you your slaves should show respect rather than fear.

Someone may say that now I am calling for slaves to have the cap of liberty and for masters to be cast down from their lofty heights when I say slaves should respect their master rather than fear him. "That is precisely what he is saying: slaves are to show respect, as if they were clients or polite visitors." A man who says such things forgets that what satisfies a god is not too little for

---

1   *mimes* Popular form of theatre in ancient Rome.

a master. The man who is respected is also loved, but love and fear cannot be mixed together.

So, in my judgment, your actions are entirely correct, for you do not wish your slaves to fear you, and you punish them with words. We use a whip to reprimand dumb beasts. Everything which offends us does not do us harm. But our fastidiousness drives us into savage rage, so that whatever does not answer our desires, brings out our anger. We wrap ourselves up in royal passions. For kings also forget their own power and the weaknesses of other men and so grow hot and boil with rage, as if they had received an injury, when the loftiness of their position keeps them completely safe from any danger. They are not unaware of this, but by complaining they seize an opportunity to harm someone. They say they have been injured in order to inflict an injury.

I do not wish to delay you any longer. For you do not need my exhortations. Among their other traits, good characters possess this quality: they make their own decisions and hold to them. Malice is fickle and changes frequently, not into something better but merely something different.

Farewell.

—c. 65 CE

Michel de Montaigne

1533–1592

Michel de Montaigne is frequently credited with creating the modern essay. He was the first to use the word "essay" (meaning "attempt" in French)
in its modern sense, applying the term to his efforts to arrive at a deeper
understanding not only of his own experience as a human being, but of the
universal experience of being human. Montaigne may have perfected the
essay—which he approached less as a form than as a technique—but he was
preceded by such ancient Roman practitioners of philosophical introspec-
tion as Plutarch, Cicero, and Seneca, all of whom figure in his masterpiece
collection, the *Essays* (1580–95). In these writings, Montaigne establishes an
intimacy with the reader such that we seem to overhear a man in conversation with himself, testing his own values, judgments, ideas, and beliefs in a
forthright spirit of skeptical inquiry.

The *Essays* do not describe the evolution of a system of thought or a theory
of knowledge, but instead explore topics as various as religious tolerance
("Of Cato the Younger"), sexual proclivities ("Of Some Verses of Virgil"),
and cultural norms ("Of Cannibals"). The result is a self-portrait of a human
being in the process of feeling, thinking, and changing. The meandering,
digressive structure of the individual pieces and the randomness of their arrangement reflect the changeful, idiosyncratic, and infinitely curious nature
of the mind in which they originated. As Montaigne observed of his project,
"I do not portray being: I portray passing."

Born to a wealthy Roman Catholic merchant, Montaigne received a thorough education in Latin, philosophy, and law, and during his lifetime held
positions as a courtier, a diplomat, a magistrate, and the mayor of Bordeaux.
The *Essays* were first translated from French into English in 1603, and were
influential in England as well as France, inspiring writers of philosophy and
of literature such as René Descartes, Francis Bacon, and William Shakespeare.

On Cannibals[1]

When king Pyrrhus[2] moved across into Italy and had scouted out the organization of the army which the Romans sent out against him, he observed, "I
do not know what sort of barbarians these are" (for the Greeks used to call all

---

1   *On Cannibals* This translation, prepared for this anthology by Ian Johnston of Vancouver Island University, is based upon the final (1595) version of the essay. Montaigne's
frequent quotations in Latin have also been translated into English.

2   *Pyrrhus* King of Epirus (306–272 BCE), northwestern Greece, who invaded Italy; despite
his skill as a general, he was eventually defeated.

foreign nations by that name) "but the formation of this army I am looking at has nothing barbarous about it." The Greeks said much the same about the army Flaminius[1] marched through their country, and so did Philip, when he looked down from a hillock on the order and layout of the Roman camp built in his kingdom under the command of Publius Sulpicius Galba.[2] There we see how we should be careful of clinging to common opinions and should judge them with the eye of reason, not by popular report.

For a long time I had with me a man who had lived ten or twelve years in that other world which was discovered in our century, in the place where Villegaignon[3] landed, which he called Antarctic France. This discovery of such an enormous country seems to merit serious consideration. I do not know if I can affirm that another such discovery will not occur in the future, given that so many people more important than we have been wrong about this one. I fear that our eyes are larger than our stomachs, that we have more curiosity than comprehension. We embrace everything, yet catch nothing but wind. Plato introduces Solon[4] telling a story which he had learned from the priests in the city of Saïs in Egypt. They said that long ago, before the Deluge,[5] there was a huge island called Atlantis, right at the entry to the Straits of Gibraltar,[6] which had more land than all of Africa and Asia combined and that the kings of this country not only possessed this island but also had extended their control so far into the mainland that they held territories across the width of Africa as far as Egypt and across Europe as far as Tuscany. They were planning to march over into Asia and to subjugate all nations bordering the Mediterranean up to the Black Sea. To achieve this they had moved across Spain, Gaul,[7] and Italy, all the way to Greece, where the Athenians stopped them. However, sometime later both the Athenians and these people, along with their island, were swallowed by the Flood.

It is very probable that this extreme inundation of water brought about strange alterations in the habitable regions of the earth, like the ones in which, so people say, the sea separated Sicily from Italy—

---

1   *Flaminius* Titus Quinctius Flaminius, Roman politician and military leader who obtained a Roman victory over Philip V of Macedon in the Second Macedonian War (200–196 BCE).

2   *Philip ... Publius Sulpicius Galba* Philip V fought against the Roman politician and general Publius Sulpicius Galba Maximus in the First Macedonian War (214–205 BCE).

3   *Villegaignon* In 1555 Nicolas Durand Villegaignon landed in the Bay of Rio de Janeiro, Brazil, and set up a French colony on a nearby island.

4   *Solon* Historical figure to whom the following story is attributed in Plato's dialogue *Critias* (fourth century BCE).

5   *Deluge* I.e., great flood; see the story of Noah in Genesis 6–8.

6   *Straits of Gibraltar* Strait at the mouth of the Mediterranean Sea.

7   *Gaul* France.

> They claim these places once were ripped apart
> by an enormously destructive force,
> where earlier both lands had been united[1]—

and split Cyprus from Syria, the island of Euboea from the mainland of Boeotia,[2] and in other places joined lands which had been separated, filling the trenches between them with sand and mud.

> ... long a sterile marsh on which men rowed
> it nourishes the neighbouring towns
> and feels the ploughshare's weight.[3]

But it does not seem very likely that this new world we have just discovered was this island of Atlantis, for it almost touched Spain, and the effect of that inundation would have been incredible if it had pushed the island back to where the new world is, a distance of more than twelve hundred leagues. Moreover, modern navigators have almost certainly already established that the new world is not an island but a mainland, connected on one side with the East Indies and on the other with the lands under the two poles. Or else, if it is divided off from them, what separates it is a narrow strait, a distance that does not entitle it to be called an island.

In these large bodies, as in our own, it appears that there are movements, some natural and others feverish. When I consider the inroads which my river, the Dordogne,[4] has made during my lifetime in the right bank of its descending flow and realize that in twenty years it has gained so much and washed away the foundations of several buildings, I clearly see that the disturbance has been extraordinary. For if it had always worked in this way or were to do so in future, the face of the earth would be completely altered. But rivers undergo changes: sometimes they overrun one bank, sometimes the other, and sometimes they flow between them. I am not speaking about sudden floods, whose causes we understand. In Medoc, along the seashore, my brother, the Sieur d'Arsac,[5] looks out at one of his estates being buried under the sand which the sea vomits up in front of her. The tops of some buildings are still visible. His rental properties and his fields have been turned into very poor pasture. The inhabitants say that for some years the sea has been pushing towards them so strongly that they have lost four leagues of ground. These sands are her harbinger: we see huge mounds of moving sand marching half a league in front

---

1   *They claim ... been united* From Virgil, *Aeneid* 3.414.
2   *Euboea* Greek island; *Boeotia* Mainland region of ancient Greece.
3   *... long ... ploughshare's weight* From Horace, *De Arte Poetica* 65.
4   *Dordogne* River that passed by Montaigne's family estate near Bordeaux, France.
5   *Medoc* Region north of Bordeaux; *Sieur d'Arsac* Lord of Arsac, a village in Medoc.

of her and overpowering the land. The other testimony from ancient times to which one could link this discovery of a new world is in Aristotle, at least if that little booklet *On Unheard-of Marvels*[1] is by him. In that work, he tells the story of certain Carthaginians[2] who, after setting out across the Atlantic Ocean beyond the Straits of Gibraltar and sailing for a long time, finally discovered a large fertile island, all covered with trees and watered by wide, deep rivers, a very long way from any mainland. Attracted by the goodness and fertility of the soil, they—and others after them—went with their wives and children and started a settlement there. However, the rulers of Carthage, noticing that their country was gradually losing its people, expressly prohibited any more people from going there, on pain of death, and they drove these new inhabitants out, fearing, so the story goes, that with the passage of time they might multiply to such an extent that they would supplant the Carthaginians themselves and ruin their state. But this story from Aristotle does not accord with our new lands any more than Plato's does.

The man I had with me was a plain, rough fellow, the sort likely to provide a true account. For intelligent people notice more and are much more curious, but they also provide their own gloss on things and, to strengthen their own interpretation and make it persuasive, they cannot help changing their story a little. They never give you a pure picture of things, but bend and disguise them to fit the view they had of them. To lend credit to their judgment and attract you to it, they willingly add to the material, stretching it out and amplifying it. We need either a very honest man or one so simple that he lacks what it takes to build up inventive falsehoods and make them plausible, someone not wedded to anything. My man was like that, and, in addition, at various times he brought some sailors and merchants he had known on that voyage to see me. Thus, I am happy with his information, without enquiring into what the cosmographers may say about it.

We need topographers who provide us a detailed account of the places they have been. But because they have seen Palestine and have that advantage over us, they wish to enjoy the privilege of telling us news about all the rest of the world. I would like everyone to write about what he knows, and only as much as he knows, not merely on this subject but on all others. For a person can have some specific knowledge of or experience with the nature of a river or a fountain and yet in other things know only what everyone else does. Yet, to publicize his small scrap of knowledge, he will undertake to write about all of physics. From this vice several serious difficulties arise.

---

1   *On Unheard-of Marvels* *De mirabilibus auscultationibus*, a text often falsely attributed to Aristotle during the sixteenth century.
2   *Carthaginians* Carthage was a major civilization in northern Africa and the Mediterranean region from the eighth to the second centuries BCE.

Now, to return to my subject, I find, from what I have been told about these people, that there is nothing barbarous and savage about them, except that everyone calls things which he does not practice himself barbaric. For, in fact, we have no test of truth and of reason other than examples and ideas of the opinions and habits in the country where we live. There we always have the perfect religion, the perfect political arrangements, the perfect and most accomplished ways of dealing with everything. Those natives are wild in the same way we call wild the fruits which nature has produced on her own in her normal manner; whereas, in fact, the ones we should really call wild are those we have altered artificially and whose ordinary behaviour we have modified. The former contain vital and vigorous virtues and properties, genuinely beneficial and natural, qualities which we have bastardized in the latter, by adapting them to gratify our corrupt taste. Nonetheless, the very flavour and delicacy in various uncultivated fruits from those countries over there are excellent even to our taste—they rival the fruit we produce. It is unreasonable that art should win the place of honour over our great and powerful mother nature. We have overburdened the beauty and richness of her works with our inventions to such an extent that we have completely suffocated her. Yet wherever she shines out in her full purity, her marvels put our vain and frivolous enterprises to shame.

> Ivy springs up better on its own
> In lonely caves arbutus grows more fair
> And birds not taught to sing have sweeter songs.[1]

All our efforts cannot succeed in recreating the nest of even the smallest bird—its texture, its beauty, and its practical convenience, let alone the web of the puny spider. All things, Plato states, are produced either by nature or by chance or by art: the greatest and most beautiful by one or other of the first two, the least and most imperfect by the last.

These nations therefore seem to me barbarous in the sense that they have received very little moulding from the human mind and are still very close to their original naive condition. Natural laws still govern them, hardly corrupted at all by our own. They live in such purity that I sometimes regret we did not learn about them earlier, at a time when there were men more capable of assessing them than we are. I am sad that Lycurgus[2] and Plato did not know them. For it seems to me that what our experience enables us to see in those nations there surpasses not only all the pictures with which poetry has embellished

1   *Ivy springs ... sweeter songs* From Propertius 1.2.10.
2   *Lycurgus* Political thinker who, according to legend, established the laws of Sparta in the eighth century BCE. It is not known whether he actually existed.

the Golden Age, as well as all its inventiveness in portraying a happy human condition, but also the conceptions and even the desires of philosophy. They have scarcely imagined such a pure and simple innocence as the one our experience reveals to us, and they would hardly have believed that our society could survive with so little artifice and social bonding among people. It is a nation, I would tell Plato, in which there is no form of commerce, no knowledge of letters, no science of numbers, no name for magistrate or political superior, no customs of servitude, no wealth or poverty, no contracts, no inheritance, no division of property, no occupations, other than leisure ones, no respect for family kinship, except for common ties, no clothing, no agriculture, no metal, no use of wine or wheat. The very words which signify lying, treason, dissimulation, avarice, envy, slander, and forgiveness are unknown. How distant from this perfection would Plato find the republic he imagined—"men freshly come from the gods."[1]

⚬   These are the habits nature first ordained.[2]

As for the rest, they live in a very pleasant and temperate country, so that, according to what my witnesses have told me, it is rare to see a sick person there. They have assured me that in this land one does not notice any of the inhabitants doddering, with rheumy eyes, toothless, or bowed down with old age. They have settled along the sea coast, closed off on the landward side by large, high mountains, with a stretch of territory about one hundred leagues wide in between. They have a great abundance of fish and meat, which has no resemblances to ours and which they simply cook and eat, without any other preparation. The first man who rode a horse there, although he had had dealings with them on several other voyages, so horrified them by his riding posture, that they killed him with arrows before they could recognize him.

Their buildings are very long, capable of holding two or three hundred souls, and covered with the bark of large trees. Strips of bark are held in the earth at one end and support and lean against one another at the top, in the style of some of our barns, in which the roof comes right down to the ground and acts as a wall. They have a wood so hard they cut with it and use it to make swords and grills to cook their meat. Their beds are made of woven cotton, suspended from the roof, like those of our sailors. Each man has his own, for the wives sleep separate from their husbands. They rise with the sun and, as soon as they get up, they eat to last them all day, for they have no other meal except that one. At that time they do not drink, like certain other Eastern

---

1   *men freshly ... the gods* From Seneca, *Letters* 90.
2   *These are ... first ordained* From Virgil, *Georgics* 2.20.

peoples Suidas[1] observed, who drank only apart from meals. They do drink several times a day and a considerable amount. The beverage is made from some root and is the colour of our claret wines. They drink it only lukewarm. It will keep for only two or three days. The drink has a slightly spicy taste, does not go to one's head, is good for the stomach, and works as a laxative for those who are not accustomed to it, but it is a very pleasant beverage for those who are. Instead of bread they use a certain white material, like preserved coriander. I have tried it—the taste is sweet and somewhat flat.

They spend the entire day dancing. Younger men go off to hunt wild animals with bows. Meanwhile, some of the women keep busy warming the drinks, which is their main responsibility. In the morning, before they begin their meal, one of the old men preaches to everyone in the whole barn, walking from one end to the other and repeating the same sentence several times until he has completed his tour of the building, which is easily one hundred paces long. He recommends only two things to them: courage against their enemies and affection for their wives. And these old men never fail to mention this obligation, adding as a refrain that their wives are the ones who keep their drinks warm and seasoned for them.

In several places, including my own home, there are examples of their beds, their ropes, their swords, their wooden bracelets, which they use to cover their wrists in combat, and their large canes open at one end, with whose sound they keep time in their dances. They are close shaven all over, and remove the hair much more cleanly than we do, using only wood or stone as a razor. They believe that the soul is immortal and that those who have deserved well of the gods are lodged in that part of the sky where the sun rises, while the damned are in regions to the west.

They have some sort of priests or prophets, who appear before the people relatively seldom, for they live in the mountains. When they arrive, there is a grand celebration and a solemn assembly of several villages (each barn, as I have described it, makes up a village, and the distance between them is approximately one French league). This prophet speaks to them in public, urging them to be virtuous and to do their duty. But their entire ethical knowledge contains only the two following articles, courage in warfare and affection for their wives. He prophesies to them about things to come and about the results they should expect from their endeavours and encourages them to go to war or to refrain from it. But he does this on the condition, that he must prophesy correctly, and if what happens to them is different from what he has predicted, he is cut up into a thousand pieces, if they catch him, and condemned as a

---

1   *Suidas* Name applied to the author of the *Suda* (10th century CE), a reference work compiling information from classical and early medieval sources.

false prophet. For this reason, a prophet who has been wrong once is never seen again.

Divination is a gift of God. For that reason, abusing it should be punished as fraud. Among the Scythians,[1] when the divines failed with their predictions, they were chained by their hands and feet, laid out on carts full of kindling and pulled by oxen, and burned there. Those who deal with matters in which the outcome depends on what human beings are capable of may be excused if they do their best. But surely the others, those who come to us with deluding assurances of an extraordinary faculty beyond our understanding, should be punished for not keeping their promises and for the recklessness of their deceit.

These natives have wars with the nations living on the other side of their mountains, further inland. They go out against them completely naked with no weapons except bows or wooden swords with a point at one end, like the tips of our hunting spears. What is astonishing is their resolution in combat, which never ends except in slaughter and bloodshed, for they have no idea of terror or flight. Each man brings back as a trophy the head of the enemy he has killed and attaches it to the entrance of his dwelling. After treating their prisoners well for a long time with every consideration they can possibly think of, the man who has a prisoner summons a grand meeting of his acquaintances. He ties a rope to one of the prisoner's arms and holds him there, gripping the other end, some paces away for fear of being injured, and he gives his dearest friend the prisoner's other arm to hold in the same way. Then the two of them, in the presence of the entire assembly, stab the prisoner to death with their swords. After that, they roast him. Then they all eat him together and send portions to their absent friends. They do this not, as people think, to nourish themselves, the way the Scythians did in ancient times, but as an act manifesting extreme vengeance. We see evidence for this from the following: having noticed that the Portuguese, who were allied with their enemies, used a different method of killing them when they took them prisoner—which was to bury them up to the waist, shoot the rest of their body full of arrows, and then hang them—they thought that this people who had come there from another world (and who had already spread the knowledge of many vicious practices throughout the neighbouring region and were much greater masters of all sorts of evil than they were) did not select this sort of vengeance for no reason and that therefore this method must be harsher than their own. And so they began to abandon their old practice and to follow this one.

---

1 *Scythians* Nomadic people who flourished in parts of Eastern Europe and Central Asia in the first millennium BCE.

I am not so much concerned that we call attention to the barbarous horror of this action as I am that, in judging their faults correctly, we should be so blind to our own. I believe that there is more barbarity in eating a man when he is alive than in eating him when he is dead, more in tearing apart by tortures and the rack a body still full of feeling, roasting it piece by piece, having it mauled and eaten by dogs and pigs (things I have not only read about but witnessed a short time ago, not among ancient enemies but among neighbours and fellow citizens, and, what is worse, under the pretext of piety and religion) than there is in roasting and eating a man once he has died.

In fact, Chrysippus and Zeno,[1] leaders of the Stoic sect, thought that there was nothing wrong in using our corpses for any purpose whatsoever, in case of need, including as a source of food, as our ancestors did when they were being besieged by Julius Caesar in the town of Alesia[2] and resolved to stave off the hunger of this siege with the bodies of old men, women, and other people useless in combat.

> They say the Gascons with such foods as these
> Prolonged their lives.[3]

And doctors are not afraid of using a dead body for all sorts of purposes in order to preserve our health, applying it either internally or externally. But no one has ever come across a point of view so unreasonable that it excuses treason, disloyalty, tyranny, and cruelty, which are common faults of ours.

Thus, we can indeed call these natives barbarians, as far as the laws of reason are concerned, but not in comparison with ourselves, who surpass them in barbarity of every kind. Their warfare is entirely noble and generous, as excusable and beautiful as this human malady can possibly be. With them it is based only on one thing, a jealous rivalry in courage. They do not argue about conquering new lands, for they still enjoy that natural fecundity which furnishes them without toil and trouble everything necessary and in such abundance that they do not need to expand their borders. They are still at that fortunate stage where they do not desire anything more than their natural demands prescribe. Everything over and above that is for them superfluous.

Those among them of the same age generally call each other brothers, those who are younger they call children, and the old men are fathers to all the others. These leave the full possession of their goods undivided to their

---

1   *Chrysippus and Zeno* Greek philosophers of the third and fourth centuries BCE.

2   *Alesia* Site of a major battle in Julius Caesar's 52 BCE invasion of Gaul (France), in which he defeated a coalition of French tribes.

3   *They say ... their lives* From Juvenal, *Satires* 15.93; *Gascons* Natives of Gascony, a southwestern region of France.

heirs in common, without any other title, except the completely simple one which nature gives to all her creatures by bringing them into the world.

If their neighbours cross the mountains to attack them and defeat them in battle, what the victors acquire is glory and the advantage of having proved themselves more courageous and valiant. For they have no further interest in the possessions of the conquered. They return to their own country, where they have no lack of anything they need, just as they do not lack that great benefit of knowing how to enjoy their condition in happiness and how to remain content with it. And the natives we are talking about, when their turn comes, do the same. They demand no ransom of their prisoners, other than a confession and a recognition that they have been beaten. But in an entire century there has not been one prisoner who did not prefer to die rather than to yield, either by his expression or by his words, a single bit of the grandeur of his invincible courage. Not one of them has been observed who did not prefer to be killed and eaten than merely to ask that he be spared. They treat the captives very freely, so that their lives will be all the more dear to them, and commonly make conversational threats about their coming death and the torments they will have to suffer, mentioning the preparations which are being made for this event, the slicing off of their limbs, and the celebrations which will be held at their expense. They do all this with one purpose in mind, to drag from the prisoners' mouths some weak or demeaning words or to make them eager to run away, in order to gain the advantage of having scared them and broken their resolution. For, all things well considered, that is the only point which makes a victory genuine.

> There is no victory
> except the one which conquers enemies who in their minds confess it.[1]

Long ago the Hungarians, who were very bellicose warriors, never pushed their advantage any further once they had made the enemy plead for mercy. For having wrung this confession from him, they let him go unharmed and without ransom, except, at most, for exacting his promise that he would not take up arms against them from that moment on.

We gain a number of advantages over our enemies which are borrowed and not our own. It is the quality of a porter, not of virtue, to have sturdier arms and legs: it is an inert and bodily quality, not an active habit. It is a stroke of luck which makes our enemy stumble and blinds his eyes with light from the sun. It is a trick of art and technique, which one may find in a worthless coward, that makes a competent fencer. The courage and value of a man lie in his heart and in his will: there one finds his true honour. Valour is strength,

---

1   *There is ... confess it* From Claudius, *On the Sixth Consulship of Honorius* 248.

not of legs and arms, but of courage and spirit. It does not consist of the value of our horse or of our weapons, but of ourselves: the man who falls still courageous and resolute, who "if his legs fail fights on his knees,"[1] who, whatever the danger of imminent death, does not relax his assertiveness one bit, and who, as he gives up his soul, still looks at his enemy with a firm and scornful eye—he is beaten, not by us but by fortune. He has been killed but not conquered. The most valiant are sometimes the most unfortunate.

Thus, there are defeats which are triumphs, as splendid as victories. Even those four sister victories, the most beautiful the eyes of the sun have ever gazed upon—Salamis, Plataea, Mycale, and Sicily[2]—never dared set all their combined glories up against the glorious defeat of king Leonidas and his men at the pass of Thermopylae.[3]

What soldier ever rushed with a more glorious and more ambitious desire to win a battle than captain Ischolas[4] did to lose one? Who has been more ingenious and more careful in ensuring his safety than he was in ensuring his own destruction. He was charged with defending a certain pass in the Peloponnese against the Arcadians.[5] Judging that this was completely impossible, given the nature of the place and the disparity in the numbers of troops, he decided that all those who confronted the enemy would have to die there. On the other hand, he thought it unworthy of his own virtue and magnanimity and of the Lacedaemonian[6] name to fail in his responsibilities. So between these two extremes he chose a middle course, as follows: he saved the youngest and most energetic of his force for the defence and service of their county, by sending them back, and he determined to hold the pass with those whose loss was less significant and by their deaths to do as much as he possibly could to make his enemies pay the highest price for their entry through it. And that is what happened. For they were soon surrounded on all sides by the Arcadians, and, after slaughtering a great many of them, he and his men were all put to the sword. Is there any trophy dedicated to the victors which would not be more deservingly given to these conquered men? A genuine victory emerges

---

1   *if his ... his knees* From Seneca, *On Providence* 2.

2   *Salamis, Plataea, Mycale* Series of Greek victories that brought an end to the second Persian invasion of Greece (480–479 BCE); *Sicily* In the First Sicilian War, also in 480 BCE, Greece defeated the attacking Carthaginians.

3   *the glorious ... of Thermopylae* During the second Persian invasion of Greece, the Spartan King Leonidas I and a hopelessly outnumbered Greek force held off the invading Persian army for several days; Leonidas and all of his soldiers died.

4   *Ischolas* Spartan commander of the fourth century BCE.

5   *Peloponnese* Peninsula in southern Greece; *Arcadians* Allied city-states of the region of Arcadia, in the Peloponnese.

6   *Lacedaemonian* Spartan.

from battle, not from survival, and virtuous honour lies in fighting, not in conquering.

To return to our story. These prisoners are so far from surrendering, in spite of everything done to them, that, by contrast, during the two or three months they are held, they look cheerful and urge their masters to hurry up and put them to the test. They defy and insult them. They reproach them with cowardice and the number of battles they have lost fighting against them. I have a song composed by one prisoner which contains a taunting invitation for them all to step up boldly and gather to dine on him, because they will at the same time be eating their fathers and grandfathers who have served to feed and nourish his body. "These muscles," he says, "this flesh, these veins—these are your own, poor fools that you are. You do not recognize that the substance of your ancestors' limbs is still contained in them. Savour them well. You will find there the taste of your own flesh"—an imaginative notion without the slightest flavour of barbarity. Those who paint these people as they die and depict what is going on when they are struck down show the prisoner spitting in the faces of his executioners and curling his lip at them in contempt. In fact, they do not stop their challenges and defiance with words and gestures right up to their final breath. Truly we have here really savage men in comparison to us. For that is what they must be beyond all doubt—either that, or we must be, for there is an amazing distance between their ways and ours.

The men there have several wives, and the higher their reputation for valour the greater the number. In their marriages there is something remarkably beautiful: with our wives jealousy deprives us of the friendship and kindness of other women, but with them a very similar jealousy leads their wives to acquire these relationships for their men. Since they care more for the honour of their husbands than for anything else, they go to great lengths to seek out and obtain as many companions for them as they can, since that is a testimony to their husbands' merit.

Our wives will cry out that this is a miracle. It is not. It is a proper marital virtue, but of the highest order. In the Bible, Leah, Rachel, Sarah, and Jacob's wives gave their beautiful servants to their husbands.[1] And Livia supported the appetites of Augustus,[2] to her own disadvantage. And Stratonice, wife of

---

1   *Leah, Rachel ... their husbands* Cf. Genesis 30. Jacob had children with his wives Rachel and Leah, as well as with their slaves Bilhah and Zilpah. Sarah, Abraham's wife, was barren, and offered her servant to Abraham as a surrogate.

2   *Livia supported ... of Augustus* Livia (58 BCE–29 CE) was the second wife of the Roman Emperor Augustus, who had a reputation as a womanizer; it was rumoured that Livia helped to find new virgins for him.

King Deiotarus[1] not only provided her husband for his own pleasure a very beautiful young housemaid in her service, but also carefully brought up her children and supported them as successors to their father's estates.

And so that people do not think that they do all this out of a simple and servile duty to habit and under pressure from the authority of their ancient customs, without reflection and judgment, because they have such stupid souls that they cannot choose any other way, I must cite some features of their capabilities. Apart from what I have just recited from one of their warrior songs, I have another, a love song which begins as follows: "Adder, stay, stay, adder, so that from the coloured markings on your skin my sister may take down the style and workmanship for a rich belt which I can give the woman I love—and in this way your beauty and your patterning will be preferred forever above all other snakes." This first couplet is the refrain of the song. Now, I am sufficiently familiar with poetry to judge this one: not only is there nothing barbaric in the imagination here, but it captures the spirit of Anacreon[2] throughout. Their language, too, is soft, with a pleasing sound, not unlike Greek in its word endings.

Three of these men, not knowing how much it will cost them one day in a loss of repose and happiness to learn about the corruptions among us and how interacting with us will lead to their ruin, which I assume is already well advanced (poor miserable creatures to let themselves be seduced by the desire for novelty and to have left the softness of their sky to come and see ours) were at Rouen when the late King Charles IX was there.[3] The king talked to them for a long time. They were shown our way of life, our splendour, and the layout of a beautiful city. After that, someone asked them their opinion, wishing to learn from them what they had found most astonishing. They answered that there were three things. I regret to say that I have forgotten the third, but I still remember two. They said, first of all, that they found it very strange that so many large, strong men with beards and weapons, who were around the king (they were probably talking about the Swiss soldiers in his guard) would agree to obey a child and that one of them was not chosen to command instead; and secondly (in their language they have a way of speaking of men as halves of one another) that they had noticed there were among us men completely

---

1   *Stratonice, wife of King Deiotarus* Stratonice is presented as a model of virtue in Plutarch's *De Mulierum Virtutibus* (*On the Bravery of Women*, first century CE); Plutarch writes that Stratonice, unable to bear children, suggested that Deiotarus secretly produce an heir for the married couple to raise as their own.

2   *Anacreon* Greek poet (c. 572–c. 488 BCE) known for his love lyrics.

3   *Three of … was there* About fifty Native Brazilians were brought to Rouen in 1550, and some were presented to King Charles IX of France (then 12 years old) when he visited Rouen in 1562.

gorged with all sorts of commodities while their other halves were beggars at their doors, emaciated by hunger and poverty. They found it strange that these needy halves could tolerate such an injustice and did not seize the others by the throat or set fire to their dwellings.

I had a really long talk with one of them, but the interpreter with me followed my meaning so badly and, because of his stupidity, had so much trouble taking in my ideas, that I got hardly anything useful from him. When I asked the native what benefit he received from his superior position among his people (for he was a captain and our sailors called him king), he told me that it was to be the first to march out into battle. How many men followed him? He pointed out to me a piece of ground to indicate that the number was as many as a space like that could hold—it might have been four or five thousand men. Did all his authority end when there was no war? He said one thing remained: when he visited the villages which depended on him, they made pathways for him through the thickets in their forest, so that he could walk along at his ease.

All this does not sound too bad. But what of that? They wear no breeches.

—1580 (revised 1595)

Jonathan Swift

1667–1745

Although the art of literary satire traces its origins to antiquity, its golden age is often said to have occurred in the late seventeenth and eighteenth centuries—the time of Molière, Dryden, Pope, and Voltaire. Among the many gifted satirical minds that set out during this period to lash the vices and follies of mankind, none was more adept than Jonathan Swift, who aimed to "vex the world" into reform but acknowledged the limitations of satire as a "glass wherein beholders do generally discover everybody's face but their own."

Swift is best known as the author of *Gulliver's Travels* (1726), but he initially rose to prominence—first with the Whigs, then with the Tories—as one of the most brilliant political writers of his day. Ordained as a priest in the Anglican Church, Swift entertained hopes for ecclesiastical preferment in England, but when in 1714 the Tory ministry fell with the death of Queen Anne, he reluctantly retreated to his native Ireland, where he had been appointed dean of St. Patrick's Cathedral in Dublin. Here Swift came face to face with the appalling conditions of the Irish poor, whose hardships were much exacerbated by English economic policy. To this day Swift is regarded as a national hero for the many letters and pamphlets—published anonymously though their authorship was generally known—in which he championed Irish political and economic independence, discharging his "savage indignation" in some of the finest prose ever written.

Swift was moved to write much of his satire in response to particular events and circumstances, but the objects of his attack—above all the moral and intellectual failings of the human race—are perennial. "A Modest Proposal" (1729), his darkest, most disturbingly cynical work, appeared at the height of Ireland's wretchedness, a time of rampant inflation, poverty, famine, homelessness, and unemployment.

A Modest Proposal

For Preventing the Children of Poor People in Ireland from Being a Burden to Their Parents or the Country, and for Making Them Beneficial to the Public

It is a melancholy object to those who walk through this great town,[1] or travel in the country, when they see the streets, the roads, and cabin doors crowded with beggars of the female sex, followed by three, four, or six children, all in

---

1 *this great town* I.e., Dublin.

rags and importuning every passenger[1] for an alms. These mothers, instead of being able to work for their honest livelihood, are forced to employ all their time in strolling[2] to beg sustenance for their helpless infants, who, as they grow up, either turn thieves for want of work, or leave their dear native country to fight for the Pretender in Spain, or sell themselves to the Barbados.[3]

I think it is agreed by all parties that this prodigious number of children in the arms, or on the backs, or at the heels of their mothers, and frequently of their fathers, is, in the present deplorable state of the kingdom, a very great additional grievance; and therefore, whoever could find out a fair, cheap, and easy method of making these children sound and useful members of the commonwealth would deserve so well of the public as to have his statue set up for a preserver of the nation.

But my intention is very far from being confined to provide only for the children of professed beggars; it is of a much greater extent, and shall take in the whole number of infants at a certain age who are born of parents in effect as little able to support them as those who demand our charity in the streets.

As to my own part, having turned my thoughts for many years upon this important subject and maturely weighed the several schemes of other projectors,[4] I have always found them grossly mistaken in their computation. 'Tis true, a child just dropped from its dam may be supported by her milk for a solar year with little other nourishment, at most not above the value of two shillings, which the mother may certainly get, or the value in scraps, by her lawful occupation of begging; and it is exactly at one year old that I propose to provide for them in such a manner as, instead of being a charge upon their parents or the parish, or wanting food and raiment for the rest of their lives, they shall on the contrary contribute to the feeding, and partly to the clothing, of many thousands.

There is likewise another great advantage in my scheme, that it will prevent those abortions, and that horrid practice of women murdering their bastard children, alas, too frequent among us, sacrificing the poor innocent babes, I doubt,[5] more to avoid the expense than the shame, which would move tears and pity in the most savage and inhuman breast.

---

1   *passenger* Passerby.

2   *strolling* Wandering, roving.

3   *the Pretender* James Francis Edward Stuart, son of James II who was deposed from the throne in the Glorious Revolution due to his overt Catholicism. Catholic Ireland was loyal to Stuart, and the Irish were often recruited by France and Spain to fight against England; *Barbados* Because of the extreme poverty in Ireland, many Irish people emigrated to the West Indies, selling their labour to sugar plantations in advance to pay for the voyage.

4   *projectors* Those who design or propose experiments or projects.

5   *doubt* Think.

The number of souls in this kingdom being usually reckoned one million and a half, of these I calculate there may be about two hundred thousand couples whose wives are breeders, from which number I subtract thirty thousand couples who are able to maintain children, although I apprehend there cannot be as many under the present distresses of the kingdom; but this being granted, there will remain one hundred and seventy thousand breeders.

I again subtract fifty thousand for those women who miscarry, or whose children die by accident or disease within the year. There only remain one hundred and twenty thousand children of poor parents annually born. The question therefore is how this number shall be reared and provided for, which, as I have already said, under the present situation of affairs is utterly impossible by all the methods hitherto proposed. For we can neither employ them in handicraft or agriculture; we neither build houses (I mean in the country) nor cultivate land.[1] They can very seldom pick up a livelihood by stealing till they arrive at six years old, except where they are of towardly parts,[2] although I confess they learn the rudiments much earlier, during which time they can however be properly looked upon only as probationers, as I have been informed by a principal gentleman in the county of Cavan, who protested to me that he never knew above one or two instances under the age of six, even in a part of the kingdom so renowned for the quickest proficiency in that art.

I am assured by our merchants that a boy or a girl before twelve years old is no saleable commodity; and even when they come to this age, they will not yield above three pounds, or three pounds and half a crown at most, on the Exchange, which cannot turn to account[3] either to the parents or the kingdom, the charge of nutriment and rags having been at least four times that value.

I shall now therefore humbly propose my own thoughts, which I hope will not be liable to the least objection.

I have been assured by a very knowing American[4] of my acquaintance in London that a young healthy child well nursed is at a year old a most delicious, nourishing, and wholesome food, whether stewed, roasted, baked, or boiled; and I make no doubt that it will equally serve in a fricassee or a ragout.[5]

I do therefore humbly offer it to public consideration that of the hundred and twenty thousand children already computed, twenty thousand may be

---

1   *neither build ... land* The British placed numerous restrictions on the Irish agricultural industry, retaining the majority of land for the grazing of sheep. The vast estates of British absentee landlords further contributed to Ireland's poverty.

2   *of towardly parts* Exceptionally able.

3   *on the Exchange* At the market; *turn to account* Result in profit.

4   *American* I.e., Native American.

5   *fricassee or a ragout* Stews.

reserved for breed, whereof only one fourth part to be males, which is more than we allow to sheep, black cattle, or swine, and my reason is that these children are seldom the fruits of marriage, a circumstance not much regarded by our savages; therefore, one male will be sufficient to serve four females. That the remaining hundred thousand may at a year old be offered in sale to the persons of quality and fortune through the kingdom, always advising the mother to let them suck plentifully of the last month, so as to render them plump and fat for a good table. A child will make two dishes at an entertainment for friends, and when the family dines alone, the fore or hind quarter will make a reasonable dish, and seasoned with a little pepper or salt will be very good boiled on the fourth day, especially in winter.

I have reckoned upon a medium that a child just born will weigh twelve pounds, and in a solar year if tolerably nursed increase to twenty-eight pounds.

I grant this food will be somewhat dear,[1] and therefore very proper for landlords, who, as they have already devoured most of the parents, seem to have the best title to the children.

Infants' flesh will be in season throughout the year, but more plentiful in March, and a little before and after. For we are told by a grave author, an eminent French physician, that, fish being a prolific[2] diet, there are more children born in Roman Catholic countries about nine months after Lent than at any other season; therefore, reckoning a year after Lent, the markets will be more glutted than usual because the number of popish[3] infants is at least three to one in this kingdom, and therefore it will have one other collateral advantage by lessening the number of papists among us.

I have already computed the charge of nursing a beggar's child (in which list I reckon all cottagers,[4] labourers, and four fifths of the farmers) to be about two shillings per annum, rags included, and I believe no gentleman would repine to give ten shillings for the carcass of a good fat child, which, as I have said, will make four dishes of excellent nutritive meat when he hath only some particular friend or his own family to dine with him. Thus the squire[5] will learn to be a good landlord and grow popular among his tenants; the mother will have eight shillings net profit and be fit for work till she produces another child.

1　*dear* Expensive.

2　*grave author* Sixteenth-century satirist François Rabelais. See his *Gargantua and Pantagruel*; *prolific* I.e., causing increased fertility.

3　*popish* Derogatory term meaning "Catholic."

4　*cottagers* Country dwellers.

5　*squire* Owner of a country estate.

Those who are more thrifty (as I must confess the times require) may flay the carcass, the skin of which, artificially[1] dressed, will make admirable gloves for ladies and summer boots for fine gentlemen.

As to our city of Dublin, shambles[2] may be appointed for this purpose in the most convenient parts of it, and butchers we may be assured will not be wanting, although I rather recommend buying the children alive and dressing them hot from the knife, as we do roasting pigs.

A very worthy person, a true lover of his country, and whose virtues I highly esteem, was lately pleased, in discoursing on this matter, to offer a refinement upon my scheme. He said that, many gentlemen of this kingdom having of late destroyed their deer, he conceived that the want of venison might be well supplied by the bodies of young lads and maidens, not exceeding fourteen years of age nor under twelve, so great a number of both sexes in every county being now ready to starve for want of work and service; and these to be disposed of by their parents if alive, or otherwise by their nearest relations. But with due deference to so excellent a friend and so deserving a patriot, I cannot be altogether in his sentiments; for as to the males, my American acquaintance assured me from frequent experience that their flesh was generally tough and lean, like that of our schoolboys, by continual exercise, and their taste disagreeable, and to fatten them would not answer the charge. Then as to the females, it would, I think with humble submission, be a loss to the public because they soon would become breeders themselves. And besides, it is not improbable that some scrupulous people might be apt to censure such a practice (although indeed very unjustly) as a little bordering upon cruelty, which, I confess, hath always been with me the strongest objection against any project, however well intended.

But in order to justify my friend, he confessed that this expedient was put into his head by the famous Psalmanazar,[3] a native of the island of Formosa, who came from thence to London above twenty years ago, and in conversation told my friend that in his country, when any young person happened to be put to death the executioner sold the carcass to persons of quality as a prime dainty, and that in his time the body of a plump girl of fifteen, who was crucified for an attempt to poison the emperor, was sold to his Imperial Majesty's Prime Minister of State and other great Mandarins of the court, in joints from the

---

1   *artificially* Artfully, skillfully.
2   *shambles* Slaughterhouses.
3   *Psalmanazar* George Psalmanazar, a French adventurer who pretended to be a Formosan and published an account of Formosan customs, *Historical and Geographical Description of Formosa* (1704), which was later exposed as fraudulent. The story Swift recounts here is found in the second edition of Psalmanazar's work.

gibbet,[1] at four hundred crowns. Neither indeed can I deny that if the same use were made of several plump young girls in this town who, without one single groat to their fortunes, cannot stir abroad without a chair,[2] and appear at the playhouse and assemblies in foreign fineries which they never will pay for, the kingdom would not be the worse.

Some persons of a desponding spirit are in great concern about that vast number of poor people who are aged, diseased, or maimed, and I have been desired to employ my thoughts what course may be taken to ease the nation of so grievous an encumbrance. But I am not in the least pain upon that matter because it is very well known that they are every day dying and rotting by cold and famine, and filth and vermin, as fast as can be reasonably expected. And as to the younger labourers, they are now in almost as hopeful a condition. They cannot get work, and consequently pine away for want of nourishment to a degree that if at any time they are accidentally hired to common labour, they have not strength to perform it; and thus the country and themselves are happily delivered from the evils to come.

I have too long digressed, and therefore shall return to my subject. I think the advantages by the proposal which I have made are obvious and many, as well as of the highest importance.

For first, as I have already observed, it would greatly lessen the number of papists, with whom we are yearly overrun, being the principal breeders of the nation as well as our most dangerous enemies, and who stay at home on purpose with a design to deliver the kingdom to the Pretender, hoping to take their advantage by the absence of so many good Protestants, who have chosen rather to leave their country than stay at home and pay tithes against their conscience to an Episcopal curate.[3]

Secondly, the poorer tenants will have something valuable of their own, which by law may be made liable to distress[4] and help to pay their landlord's rent, their corn and cattle being already seized, and money a thing unknown.

Thirdly, whereas the maintenance of an hundred thousand children from two years old and upwards cannot be computed at less than ten shillings apiece per annum, the nation's stock will be thereby increased fifty thousand pounds per annum, besides the profit of a new dish introduced to the tables of all gentlemen of fortune in the kingdom who have any refinement in taste,

---

1   *gibbet* Gallows.

2   *groat* Silver coin equal in value to four pence. It was removed from circulation in 1662, and thereafter "a groat" was used metaphorically to signify any very small sum; *chair* Sedan chair, which seated one person and was carried on poles by two men.

3   *Episcopal curate* I.e., Anglican church official.

4   *distress* Seizure of property for the payment of debt.

and the money will circulate among ourselves, the goods being entirely of our own growth and manufacture.

Fourthly, the constant breeders, besides the gain of eight shillings sterling per annum by the sale of their children, will be rid of the charge of maintaining them after the first year.

Fifthly, this food would likewise bring great customs to taverns, where the vintners will certainly be so prudent as to procure the best receipts[1] for dressing it to perfection, and consequently have their houses frequented by all the fine gentlemen who justly value themselves upon their knowledge in good eating. And a skillful cook who understands how to oblige his guests will contrive to make it as expensive as they please.

Sixthly, this would be a great inducement to marriage, which all wise nations have either encouraged by rewards or enforced by laws and penalties. It would increase the care and tenderness of mothers toward their children, when they were sure of a settlement for life to the poor babes, provided in some sort by the public, to their annual profit instead of expense. We should soon see an honest emulation[2] among the married women, which of them could bring the fattest child to market. Men would become as fond of their wives during the time of their pregnancy as they are now of their mares in foal, their cows in calf, or sows when they are ready to farrow, nor offer to beat or kick them (as it is too frequent a practice) for fear of a miscarriage.

Many other advantages might be enumerated: for instance, the addition of some thousand carcasses in our exportation of barrelled beef; the propagation of swine's flesh and improvement in the art of making good bacon, so much wanted among us by the great destruction of pigs, too frequent at our tables, which are no way comparable in taste or magnificence to a well-grown, fat yearling child, which, roasted whole, will make a considerable figure at a Lord Mayor's feast or any other public entertainment. But this and many others I omit, being studious of brevity.

Supposing that one thousand families in this city would be constant customers for infants' flesh, besides others who might have it at merry-meetings, particularly weddings and christenings, I compute that Dublin would take off annually about twenty thousand carcasses, and the rest of the kingdom (where probably they will be sold somewhat cheaper) the remaining eighty thousand.

I can think of no one objection that will possibly be raised against this proposal, unless it should be urged that the number of people will be thereby much lessened in the kingdom. This I freely own, and it was indeed one principal design in offering it to the world. I desire the reader will observe

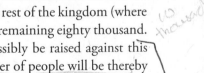

---

1   *receipts* Recipes.
2   *emulation* Rivalry.

that I calculate my remedy for this one individual kingdom of Ireland, and for no other that ever was, is, or, I think, ever can be upon earth. Therefore let no man talk to me of other expedients:[1] of taxing our absentees at five shillings a pound; of using neither clothes nor household furniture, except what is of our own growth and manufacture; of utterly rejecting the materials and instruments that promote foreign luxury; of curing the expensiveness of pride, vanity, idleness, and gaming[2] in our women; of introducing a vein of parsimony, prudence, and temperance; of learning to love our country, wherein we differ even from Laplanders and the inhabitants of Topinamboo; of quitting our animosities and factions, nor act any longer like the Jews, who were murdering one another at the very moment their city was taken;[3] of being a little cautious not to sell our country and consciences for nothing; of teaching landlords to have at least one degree of mercy toward their tenants; lastly, of putting a spirit of honesty, industry, and skill into our shopkeepers, who, if a resolution could now be taken to buy only our native goods, would immediately unite to cheat and exact upon us in the price, the measure, and the goodness, nor could ever yet be brought to make one fair proposal of just dealing, though often in earnest invited to it.

Therefore I repeat, let no man talk to me of these and the like expedients till he hath at least some glimpse of hope that there will ever be some hearty and sincere attempt to put them in practice.

But as to myself, having been wearied out for many years with offering vain, idle, visionary thoughts, and at length utterly despairing of success, I fortunately fell upon this proposal, which, as it is wholly new, so it hath something solid and real, of no expense and little trouble, full in our own power, and whereby we can incur no danger in disobliging England. For this kind of commodity will not bear exportation, the flesh being of too tender a consistence to admit a long continuance in salt, although perhaps I could name a country[4] which would be glad to eat up our whole nation without it.

After all, I am not so violently bent upon my own opinion as to reject any offer, proposed by wise men, which shall be found equally innocent, cheap, easy, and effectual. But before something of that kind shall be advanced in

---

1   *other expedients* All of which Swift had already proposed in earnest attempts to remedy Ireland's poverty. See, for example, his *Proposal for the Universal Use of Irish Manufactures.* In early editions the following proposals were italicized to show the suspension of Swift's ironic tone.

2   *gaming* Gambling.

3   *Topinamboo* District in Brazil; *Jews ... was taken* According to the history of Flavius Josephus, Roman Emperor Titus's invasion and capture of Jerusalem in 70 BCE was aided by the fact that factional fighting had divided the city.

4   *a country* I.e., England.

asks for counter argument.

contradiction to my scheme, and offering a better, I desire the author or authors will be pleased maturely to consider two points.

First, as things now stand, how they will be able to find food and raiment for one hundred thousand useless mouths and backs.

And secondly, there being a round million of creatures in human figure throughout this kingdom whose whole subsistence, put into a common stock, would leave them in debt two million of pounds sterling, adding those who are beggars by profession to the bulk of farmers, cottagers, and labourers with their wives and children, who are beggars in effect.

I desire those politicians who dislike my overture, and may perhaps be so bold to attempt an answer, that they will first ask the parents of these mortals whether they would not at this day think it a great happiness to have been sold for food at a year old in the manner I prescribe, and thereby have avoided such a perpetual scene of misfortunes as they have since gone through by the oppression of landlords, the impossibility of paying rent without money or trade, the want of common sustenance, with neither house nor clothes to cover them from the inclemencies of the weather, and the most inevitable prospect of entailing[1] the like or greater miseries upon their breed forever.

I profess in the sincerity of my heart that I have not the least personal interest in endeavoring to promote this necessary work, having no other motive than the public good of my country by advancing our trade, providing for infants, relieving the poor, and giving some pleasure to the rich. I have no children by which I can propose to get a single penny, the youngest being nine years old, and my wife past childbearing.

—1729

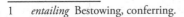

1   *entailing* Bestowing, conferring.

Percy Bysshe Shelley
1792–1822

A poet, thinker, and activist devoted to social reform and the overthrow of injustice, Percy Shelley was not only one of the most radical English Romantics but—as even the comparatively conservative Wordsworth acknowledged—"one of the best *artists* of us all ... in workmanship of style." Shelley's politics and poetics intersect in visionary works that seek to stimulate in the reader an awareness of a higher order of experience and greater forms of value than a materialist conception of the world can comprehend. His critics dismissed him as a reckless naïf with "a weak grasp upon the actual," but his idealism was bounded by his skepticism, and what he called his "dreams of what ought to be" take greater heed in his mature works of "the difficult and unbending realities of actual life."

For much of his life Shelley saw himself as a persecuted outcast. In light of his atheism and political views, his scandalous espousal of free love, and his sympathy for early democratic thinkers such as Thomas Paine and William Godwin, his work was often suppressed or attacked. Shelley was frequently on the defensive, not only with respect to his character and work but on behalf of poetry itself. His unfinished *Defence of Poetry* (1840), written to rebut a tongue-in-cheek essay in which his friend Thomas Love Peacock declared the art useless in the modern era of technological and scientific progress, remains an eloquent vindication of the transformative power of the "poetical faculty" and the social and moral role of the poet.

from *A Defence of Poetry, or Remarks Suggested by an Essay Entitled "The Four Ages of Poetry"* [1]

According to one mode of regarding those two classes of mental action which are called reason and imagination, the former may be considered as mind con-

---

1   *A Defence ... Ages of Poetry* This essay, begun in 1822 and never completed, was written in response to an 1820 essay by Shelley's friend Thomas Love Peacock called "The Four Ages of Poetry." In this partially ironic essay, Peacock describes four cycles through which poetry passes: the first is an iron age of crude folk ballads, medieval romances, etc.; the second, the gold age, contains the great epics of Homer, Dante, and Milton; the third, the silver age, contains the "derivative" poetry of the Augustan poets (who included John Dryden and Alexander Pope); and the fourth stage, the age of brass, is that of Peacock's contemporaries, whom he claimed were markedly inferior. Criticizing Romantic poets such as Byron, Coleridge, and Wordsworth, Peacock urged the men of his generation to apply themselves to new sciences, such as astronomy, economics, politics, mathematics,

templating the relations borne by one thought to another, however produced; and the latter, as mind acting upon those thoughts so as to colour them with its own light, and composing from them, as from elements, other thoughts, each containing within itself the principle of its own integrity. The one is the τὸ ποιειϖ,[1] or the principle of synthesis, and has for its objects those forms which are common to universal nature and existence itself; the other is the τὸ λογιζειϖ[2] or principle of analysis, and its action regards the relations of things, simply as relations; considering thoughts, not in their integral unity, but as the algebraical representations which conduct to certain general results. Reason is the enumeration of quantities already known; imagination is the perception of the value of those quantities, both separately and as a whole. Reason respects the differences, and imagination the similitudes of things. Reason is to Imagination as the instrument to the agent, as the body to the spirit, as the shadow to the substance.

Poetry, in a general sense, may be defined to be "the expression of the Imagination": and poetry is connate with the origin of man. Man is an instrument over which a series of external and internal impressions are driven, like the alternations of an ever-changing wind over an Æolian lyre,[3] which move it by their motion to ever-changing melody. But there is a principle within the human being, and perhaps within all sentient beings, which acts otherwise than in the lyre, and produces not melody alone, but harmony, by an internal adjustment of the sounds or motions thus excited to the impressions which excite them. It is as if the lyre could accommodate its chords to the motions of that which strikes them, in a determined proportion of sound; even as the musician can accommodate his voice to the sound of the lyre. A child at play by itself will express its delight by its voice and motions; and every inflexion of tone and every gesture will bear exact relation to a corresponding antitype in the pleasurable impressions which awakened it; it will be the reflected image of that impression; and as the lyre trembles and sounds after the wind has died away, so the child seeks, by prolonging in its voice and motions the duration of the effect, to prolong also a consciousness of the cause. In relation to the objects which delight a child, these expressions are what poetry is to higher objects. The savage (for the savage is to ages what the child is to years) expresses

---

or chemistry, instead of poetry. Though Shelley recognized Peacock's satirical humour, he also acknowledged that Peacock had put his finger on a common bias of the time—both in the theories of Utilitarian philosophers and in general public opinion—in favour of economic growth and scientific progress over creativity and humanitarian concerns. It was this bias that he attempted to correct in his *Defence*.

1   τὸ ποιειϖ   Greek: making.
2   τὸ λογιζειϖ   Greek: reasoning.
3   *Æolian lyre*   Stringed instrument that produces music when exposed to wind.

the emotions produced in him by surrounding objects in a similar manner; and language and gesture, together with plastic[1] or pictorial imitation, become the image of the combined effect of those objects, and of his apprehension of them. Man in society, with all his passions and his pleasures, next becomes the object of the passions and pleasures of man; an additional class of emotions produces an augmented treasure of expressions; and language, gesture, and the imitative arts become at once the representation and the medium, the pencil and the picture, the chisel and the statue, the chord and the harmony. The social sympathies, or those laws from which as from its elements society results, begin to develop themselves from the moment that two human beings coexist; the future is contained within the present as the plant within the seed; and equality, diversity, unity, contrast, mutual dependence, become the principles alone capable of affording the motives according to which the will of a social being is determined to action, inasmuch as he is social; and constitute pleasure in sensation, virtue in sentiment, beauty in art, truth in reasoning, and love in the intercourse of kind. Hence men, even in the infancy of society, observe a certain order in their words and actions, distinct from that of the objects and the impressions represented by them, all expression being subject to the laws of that from which it proceeds. But let us dismiss those more general considerations which might involve an enquiry into the principles of society itself, and restrict our view to the manner in which the imagination is expressed upon its forms.

In the youth of the world, men dance and sing and imitate natural objects, observing[2] in these actions, as in all others, a certain rhythm or order. And, although all men observe a similar, they observe not the same order, in the motions of the dance, in the melody of the song, in the combinations of language, in the series of their imitations of natural objects. For there is a certain order or rhythm belonging to each of these classes of mimetic representation, from which the hearer and the spectator receive an intenser and purer pleasure than from any other: the sense of an approximation to this order has been called taste, by modern writers. Every man in the infancy of art observes an order which approximates more or less closely to that from which this highest delight results: but the diversity is not sufficiently marked, as that its gradations should be sensible, except in those instances where the predominance of this faculty of approximation to the beautiful (for so we may be permitted to name the relation between this highest pleasure and its cause) is very great. Those in whom it exists in excess are poets, in the most universal sense of the word; and the pleasure resulting from the manner in which they express the influence of

---

1   *plastic* I.e., sculptural.
2   *observing* Following.

society or nature upon their own minds, communicates itself to others, and gathers a sort of reduplication from that community. Their language is vitally metaphorical; that is, it marks the before unapprehended relations of things, and perpetuates their apprehension, until the words which represent them, become through time signs for portions or classes of thoughts instead of pictures of integral thoughts; and then if no new poets should arise to create afresh the associations which have been thus disorganized, language will be dead to all the nobler purposes of human intercourse. These similitudes or relations are finely said by Lord Bacon to be "the same footsteps of nature impressed upon the various subjects of the world"[1]—and he considers the faculty which perceives them as the storehouse of axioms common to all knowledge. In the infancy of society every author is necessarily a poet, because language itself is poetry; and to be a poet is to apprehend the true and the beautiful, in a word the good which exists in the relation, subsisting, first between existence and perception, and secondly between perception and expression. Every original language near to its source is in itself the chaos of a cyclic poem:[2] the copiousness of lexicography and the distinctions of grammar are the works of a later age, and are merely the catalogue and the form of the creations of Poetry.

But Poets, or those who imagine and express this indestructible order, are not only the authors of language and of music, of the dance and architecture and statuary and painting: they are the institutors of laws, and the founders of civil society and the inventors of the arts of life and the teachers, who draw into a certain propinquity with the beautiful and the true that partial apprehension of the agencies of the invisible world which is called religion. Hence all original religions are allegorical, or susceptible of allegory, and like Janus have a double face of false and true.[3] Poets, according to the circumstances of the age and nation in which they appeared, were called in the earlier epochs of the world legislators or prophets:[4] a poet essentially comprises and unites both these characters. For he not only beholds intensely the present as it is, and discovers those laws according to which present things ought to be ordered, but he beholds the future in the present, and his thoughts are the germs of the flower and the fruit of latest time. Not that I assert poets to be prophets in the gross sense of the word, or that they can foretell the form as surely as

---

1   *the same ... world* From Francis Bacon's *Of the Advancement of Learning* (1605) 3.1.
2   *cyclic poem* Set of poems dealing with the same subject (though not always by the same author). The "Arthurian Cycle," a series of poems about the court of King Arthur, is one example of the genre.
3   *like Janus ... true* Janus, the Roman god of war, of doorways, and of beginnings and endings, is generally depicted with two faces, one looking forward and one back.
4   *were called ... prophets* See Sir Philip Sidney's *Defence of Poesy* (1595), in which he points out that *vates*, the Latin word for poet, also means diviner or prophet.

they foreknow the spirit of events: such is the pretence of superstition which would make poetry an attribute of prophecy, rather than prophecy an attribute of poetry. A Poet participates in the eternal, the infinite, and the one; as far as relates to his conceptions, time and place and number are not. The grammatical forms which express the moods of time, and the difference of persons and the distinction of place, are convertible with respect to the highest poetry without injuring it as poetry, and the choruses of Æschylus, and the book of Job, and Dante's Paradise[1] would afford, more than any other writings, examples of this fact, if the limits of this essay did not forbid citation. The creations of sculpture, painting, and music are illustrations still more decisive.

Language, colour, form, and religious and civil habits of action are all the instruments and materials of poetry; they may be called poetry by that figure of speech which considers the effect as a synonym of the cause. But poetry in a more restricted sense expresses those arrangements of language, and especially metrical language, which are created by that imperial faculty whose throne is curtained within the invisible nature of man. And this springs from the nature itself of language, which is a more direct representation of the actions and passions of our internal being, and is susceptible of more various and delicate combinations, than colour, form, or motion, and is more plastic and obedient to the control of that faculty of which it is the creation. For language is arbitrarily produced by the Imagination and has relation to thoughts alone; but all other materials, instruments and conditions of art, have relations among each other, which limit and interpose between conception and expression. The former is as a mirror which reflects, the latter as a cloud which enfeebles, the light of which both are mediums of communication. Hence the fame of sculptors, painters and musicians, although the intrinsic powers of the great masters of these arts, may yield in no degree to that of those who have employed language as the hieroglyphic of their thoughts, has never equalled that of poets in the restricted sense of the term; as two performers of equal skill will produce unequal effects from a guitar and a harp. The fame of legislators and founders of religions, so long as their institutions last, alone seems to exceed that of poets in the restricted sense; but it can scarcely be a question whether, if we deduct the celebrity which their flattery of the gross opinions of the vulgar usually conciliates, together with that which belonged to them in their higher character of poets, any excess will remain.

We have thus circumscribed the meaning of the word Poetry within the limits of that art which is the most familiar and the most perfect expression of

---

1   *Æschylus* Greek tragic dramatist (c. 525–456 BCE); *Dante's Paradise* Reference to Italian poet Dante Alighieri's fourteenth-century work *The Divine Comedy*, which describes a journey from Hell, through Purgatory, to Paradise.

the faculty itself. It is necessary however to make the circle still narrower, and to determine the distinction between measured and unmeasured language; for the popular division into prose and verse is inadmissible in accurate philosophy. Sounds as well as thoughts have relation both between each other and towards that which they represent, and a perception of the order of those relations has always been found connected with a perception of the order of the relations of thoughts. Hence the language of poets has ever affected a certain uniform and harmonious recurrence of sound, without which it were not poetry, and which is scarcely less indispensable to the communication of its influence, than the words themselves, without reference to that peculiar order....

A poem is the very image of life expressed in its eternal truth. There is this difference between a story and a poem, that a story is a catalogue of detached facts, which have no other bond of connection than time, place, circumstance, cause and effect; the other is the creation of actions according to the unchangeable forms of human nature, as existing in the mind of the creator, which is itself the image of all other minds. The one is partial, and applies only to a definite period of time, and a certain combination of events which can never again recur; the other is universal, and contains within itself the germ of a relation to whatever motives or actions have place in the possible varieties of human nature....

Poetry is ever accompanied with pleasure: all spirits on which it falls open themselves to receive the wisdom which is mingled with its delight. In the infancy of the world, neither poets themselves nor their auditors are fully aware of the excellence of poetry: for it acts in a divine and unapprehended manner, beyond and above consciousness; and it is reserved for future generations to contemplate and measure the mighty cause and effect in all the strength and splendour of their union. Even in modern times, no living poet ever arrived at the fullness of his fame; the jury which sits in judgment upon a poet, belonging as he does to all time, must be composed of his peers: it must be impanelled by Time from the selectest of the wise of many generations. A Poet is a nightingale, who sits in darkness and sings to cheer its own solitude with sweet sounds; his auditors are as men entranced by the melody of an unseen musician, who feel that they are moved and softened, yet know not whence or why. The poems of Homer and his contemporaries were the delight of infant Greece; they were the elements of that social system which is the column upon which all succeeding civilization has reposed. Homer embodied the ideal perfection of his age in human character; nor can we doubt that those who read his verses were awakened to an ambition of becoming like to Achilles, Hector and Ulysses:[1] the truth and beauty of friendship, patriotism, and persevering devotion to an

---

1   *Achilles, Hector and Ulysses* Trojan and Greek heroes in Homer's *Iliad* and *Odyssey*.

object were unveiled to the depths in these immortal creations: the sentiments of the auditors must have been refined and enlarged by a sympathy with such great and lovely impersonations, until from admiring they imitated, and from imitation they identified themselves with the objects of their admiration....

The whole objection, however, of the immorality of poetry[1] rests upon a misconception of the manner in which poetry acts to produce the moral improvement of man. Ethical science[2] arranges the elements which poetry has created, and propounds schemes and proposes examples of civil and domestic life: nor is it for want of admirable doctrines that men hate, and despise, and censure, and deceive, and subjugate one another. But Poetry acts in another and diviner manner. It awakens and enlarges the mind itself by rendering it the receptacle of a thousand unapprehended combinations of thought. Poetry lifts the veil from the hidden beauty of the world, and makes familiar objects be as if they were not familiar; it reproduces all that it represents, and the impersonations clothed in its Elysian[3] light stand thenceforward in the minds of those who have once contemplated them, as memorials of that gentle and exalted content which extends itself over all thoughts and actions with which it coexists. The great secret of morals is Love; or a going out of our own nature, and an identification of ourselves with the beautiful which exists in thought, action, or person not our own. A man, to be greatly good, must imagine intensely and comprehensively; he must put himself in the place of another and of many others; the pains and pleasures of his species must become his own. The great instrument of moral good is the imagination; and poetry administers to the effect by acting upon the cause. Poetry enlarges the circumference of the imagination by replenishing it with thoughts of ever new delight, which have the power of attracting and assimilating to their own nature all other thoughts, and which form new intervals and interstices whose void for ever craves fresh food. Poetry strengthens that faculty which is the organ of the moral nature of man, in the same manner as exercise strengthens a limb. A Poet therefore would do ill to embody his own conceptions of right and wrong, which are usually those of his place and time, in his poetical creations, which participate in neither. By this assumption of the inferior office of interpreting the effect, in which perhaps after all he might acquit himself but imperfectly, he would resign the glory in a participation in the cause. There was little danger that Homer, or any of the eternal poets, should have so far misunderstood themselves as to have abdicated this throne of their widest dominion. Those

---

1   *immorality of poetry* An objection voiced by Plato in his *Republic*, in which he says that poetry often depicts characters who are morally imperfect and whose actions do not provide suitable examples for readers.

2   *Ethical science* Moral philosophy.

3   *reproduces* I.e., produces or creates anew; *Elysian* I.e., of paradise.

in whom the poetical faculty, though great, is less intense, as Euripides, Lucan, Tasso, Spenser,[1] have frequently affected a moral aim, and the effect of their poetry is diminished in exact proportion to the degree in which they compel us to advert to this purpose....

The drama at Athens, or wheresoever else it may have approached to its perfection, coexisted with the moral and intellectual greatness of the age. The tragedies of the Athenian poets are as mirrors in which the spectator beholds himself, under a thin disguise of circumstance, stript of all but that ideal perfection and energy which every one feels to be the internal type of all that he loves, admires, and would become. The imagination is enlarged by a sympathy with pains and passions so mighty that they distend in their conception the capacity of that by which they are conceived; the good affections are strengthened by pity, indignation, terror and sorrow; and an exalted calm is prolonged from the satiety of this high exercise of them into the tumult of familiar life; even crime is disarmed of half its horror and all its contagion by being represented as the fatal consequence of the unfathomable agencies of nature; error is thus divested of its willfulness; men can no longer cherish it as the creation of their choice. In a drama of the highest order there is little food for censure or hatred; it teaches rather self-knowledge and self-respect. Neither the eye nor the mind can see itself, unless reflected upon that which it resembles. The drama, so long as it continues to express poetry, is as a prismatic and many-sided mirror, which collects the brightest rays of human nature and divides and reproduces them from the simplicity of these elementary forms, and touches them with majesty and beauty, and multiplies all that it reflects, and endows it with the power of propagating its like wherever it may fall.

But in periods of the decay of social life, the drama sympathizes with that decay. Tragedy becomes a cold imitation of the form of the great masterpieces of antiquity, divested of all harmonious accompaniment of the kindred arts; and often the very form misunderstood: or a weak attempt to teach certain doctrines, which the writer considers as moral truths; and which are usually no more than specious flatteries of some gross vice or weakness with which the author in common with his auditors are infected....

The drama being that form under which a greater number of modes of expression of poetry are susceptible of being combined than any other, the connection of poetry and social good is more observable in the drama than in whatever other form: and it is indisputable that the highest perfection of human society has ever corresponded with the highest dramatic excellence;

---

1   *Euripides* Greek tragedian of the fifth century BCE; *Lucan* Roman poet of the first century CE; *Tasso* Torquato Tasso, Italian epic poet of the sixteenth century; *Spenser* Edmund Spenser, sixteenth-century epic poet; author of *The Faerie Queene*.

and that the corruption or the extinction of the drama in a nation where it has once flourished, is a mark of a corruption of manners, and an extinction of the energies which sustain the soul of social life. But, as Machiavelli[1] says of political institutions, that life may be preserved and renewed, if men should arise capable of bringing back the drama to its principles. And this is true with respect to poetry in its most extended sense: all language, institution and form, require not only to be produced but to be sustained: the office and character of a poet participates in the divine nature as regards providence, no less than as regards creation.

… It is admitted that the exercise of the imagination is most delightful, but it is alleged that that of reason is more useful. Let us examine as the grounds of this distinction, what is here meant by Utility. Pleasure or good, in a general sense, is that which the consciousness of a sensitive and intelligent being seeks, and in which when found it acquiesces. There are two kinds of pleasure, one durable, universal, and permanent; the other transitory and particular. Utility may either express the means of producing the former or the latter. In the former sense, whatever strengthens and purifies the affections, enlarges the imagination, and adds spirit to sense, is useful. But the meaning in which the Author of the Four Ages of Poetry seems to have employed the word utility is the narrower one of banishing the importunity of the wants of our animal nature, the surrounding men with security of life, the dispersing the grosser delusions of superstition, and the conciliating such a degree of mutual forbearance among men as may consist with the motives of personal advantage.

Undoubtedly the promoters of utility in this limited sense have their appointed office in society. They follow the footsteps of poets, and copy the sketches of their creations into the book of common life. They make space, and give time. Their exertions are of the highest value so long as they confine their administration of the concerns of the inferior powers of our nature within the limits due to the superior ones. But whilst the skeptic destroys gross superstitions, let him spare to deface, as some of the French writers have defaced, the eternal truths charactered upon the imaginations of men. Whilst the mechanist abridges, and the political economist combines, labour, let them beware that their speculations, for want of correspondence with those first principles which belong to the imagination, do not tend, as they have in modern England, to exasperate at once the extremes of luxury and want. They have exemplified the saying, "To him that hath, more shall be given; and from him that hath not,

---

1   *Machiavelli* Niccolò Machiavelli (1469–1527), author of the political treatise *The Prince.*

the little that he hath shall be taken away."[1] The rich have become richer, and the poor have become poorer; and the vessel of the state is driven between the Scylla and Charybdis[2] of anarchy and despotism. Such are the effects which must ever flow from an unmitigated exercise of the calculating faculty.

It is difficult to define pleasure in its highest sense; the definition involving a number of apparent paradoxes. For, from an inexplicable defect of harmony in the constitution of human nature, the pain of the inferior is frequently connected with the pleasures of the superior portions of our being. Sorrow, terror, anguish, despair itself are often the chosen expressions of an approximation to the highest good. Our sympathy in tragic fiction depends on this principle; tragedy delights by affording a shadow of the pleasure which exists in pain. This is the source also of the melancholy which is inseparable from the sweetest melody. The pleasure that is in sorrow is sweeter than the pleasure of pleasure itself. And hence the saying, "It is better to go to the house of mourning, than to the house of mirth."[3] Not that this highest species of pleasure is necessarily linked with pain. The delight of love and friendship, the ecstasy of the admiration of nature, the joy of the perception and still more of the creation of poetry is often wholly unalloyed.

The production and assurance of pleasure in this highest sense is true utility. Those who produce and preserve this pleasure are Poets or poetical philosophers.

The exertions of Locke, Hume, Gibbon, Voltaire, Rousseau,[4] and their disciples, in favour of oppressed and deluded humanity, are entitled to the gratitude of mankind. Yet it is easy to calculate the degree of moral and intellectual improvement which the world would have exhibited, had they never lived. A little more nonsense would have been talked for a century or two; and perhaps a few more men, women, and children, burnt as heretics. We might not at this moment have been congratulating each other on the abolition of the Inquisition in Spain.[5] But it exceeds all imagination to conceive what would have been the moral condition of the world if neither Dante, Petrarch, Boccaccio, Chaucer, Shakespeare, Calderon, Lord Bacon, nor Milton, had ever

---

1   *To him ... away* Repeatedly said by Jesus (Matthew 25.29, Mark 4.25, Luke 8.18 and 19.26).

2   *Scylla and Charybdis* A group of rocks and a whirlpool located at the Strait of Messina (between Sicily and mainland Italy).

3   *It is ... mirth* From Ecclesiastes 7.2.

4   *Locke ... Rousseau* John Locke, David Hume, Edward Gibbon, François-Marie Arouet Voltaire, and Jean-Jacques Rousseau, noted philosophers of the seventeenth and eighteenth centuries.

5   *We might ... Spain* The Inquisition was suspended in 1820, the year before Shelley wrote this essay, and abolished permanently in 1834.

existed; if Raphael and Michael Angelo[1] had never been born; if the Hebrew poetry had never been translated; if a revival of the study of Greek literature had never taken place; if no monuments of ancient sculpture had been handed down to us; and if the poetry of the religion of the ancient world had been extinguished together with its belief. The human mind could never, except by the intervention of these excitements, have been awakened to the invention of the grosser sciences, and that application of analytical reasoning to the aberrations of society, which it is now attempted to exalt over the direct expression of the inventive and creative faculty itself.

... The cultivation of those sciences which have enlarged the limits of the empire of man over the external world, has, for want of the poetical faculty, proportionally circumscribed those of the internal world; and man, having enslaved the elements, remains himself a slave. To what but a cultivation of the mechanical arts in a degree disproportioned to the presence of the creative faculty, which is the basis of all knowledge, is to be attributed the abuse of all invention for abridging and combining labour, to the exasperation of the inequality of mankind? From what other cause has it arisen that the discoveries which should have lightened, have added a weight to the curse imposed on Adam?[2] Poetry, and the principle of Self, of which money is the visible incarnation, are the God and the Mammon of the world.[3]

The functions of the poetical faculty are two-fold; by one it creates new materials of knowledge, and power and pleasure; by the other it engenders in the mind a desire to reproduce and arrange them according to a certain rhythm and order which may be called the beautiful and the good. The cultivation of poetry is never more to be desired than at periods when, from an excess of the selfish and calculating principle, the accumulation of the materials of external life exceed the quantity of the power of assimilating them to the internal laws of human nature. The body has then become too unwieldy for that which animates it.

Poetry is indeed something divine. It is at once the centre and circumference of knowledge; it is that which comprehends all science, and that to which all science must be referred. It is at the same time the root and blossom of all other systems of thought: it is that from which all spring, and that which

---

1   *Petrarch* Fourteenth-century Italian poet, best known for developing the Italian/Petrarchan sonnet; *Boccaccio* Italian poet, author of the *Decameron* (1351–53); *Calderon* Seventeenth-century Spanish poet and dramatist; *Raphael and Michael Angelo* Italian Renaissance painters.
2   *curse imposed on Adam* Adam is cursed to labour for his food; see Genesis 3.17–19.
3   *God and ... world* See Matthew 6.24: "No man can serve two masters: for either he will hate the one, and love the other; or else he will hold to the one, and despise the other. Ye cannot serve God and Mammon," Mammon being the false idol of worldly possessions.

adorns all; and that which, if blighted, denies the fruit and the seed, and withholds from the barren world the nourishment and the succession of the scions[1] of the tree of life. It is the perfect and consummate surface and bloom of things; it is as the odour and the colour of the rose to the texture of the elements which compose it, as the form and the splendour of unfaded beauty to the secrets of anatomy and corruption. What were Virtue, Love, Patriotism, Friendship &c.—what were the scenery of this beautiful Universe which we inhabit—what were our consolations on this side of the grave—and what were our aspirations beyond it—if Poetry did not ascend to bring light and fire from those eternal regions where the owl-winged faculty of calculation dare not ever soar? Poetry is not like reasoning, a power to be exerted according to the determination of the will. A man cannot say, "I will compose poetry." The greatest poet even cannot say it: for the mind in creation is as a fading coal which some invisible influence, like an inconstant wind, awakens to transitory brightness: this power arises from within, like the colour of a flower which fades and changes as it is developed, and the conscious portions of our natures are unprophetic either of its approach or its departure.…

Poetry is the record of the best and happiest moments of the happiest and best minds. We are aware of evanescent visitations of thought and feeling sometimes associated with place or person, sometimes regarding our own mind alone, and always arising unforeseen and departing unbidden, but elevating and delightful beyond all expression: so that even in the desire and the regret they leave, there cannot but be pleasure, participating as it does in the nature of its object. It is as it were the interpenetration of a diviner nature through our own; but its footsteps are like those of a wind over a sea, which the coming calm erases, and whose traces remain only as on the wrinkled sand which paves it. These and corresponding conditions of being are experienced principally by those of the most delicate sensibility and the most enlarged imagination; and the state of mind produced by them is at war with every base desire. The enthusiasm of virtue, love, patriotism, and friendship is essentially linked with these emotions; and whilst they last, self appears as what it is, an atom to a Universe. Poets are not only subject to these experiences as spirits of the most refined organization, but they can colour all that they combine with the evanescent hues of this ethereal world; a word, a trait in the representation of a scene or a passion, will touch the enchanted chord, and reanimate, in those who have ever experienced these emotions, the sleeping, the cold, the buried image of the past. Poetry thus makes immortal all that is best and most beautiful in the world; it arrests the vanishing apparitions which haunt

---

1   *scions* Shoots.

the interlunations[1] of life, and veiling them or in language or in form sends them forth among mankind, bearing sweet news of kindred joy to those with whom their sisters abide—abide, because there is no portal of expression from the caverns of the spirit which they inhabit into the universe of things. Poetry redeems from decay the visitations of the divinity in man.

Poetry turns all things to loveliness; it exalts the beauty of that which is most beautiful, and it adds beauty to that which is most deformed: it marries exultation and horror, grief and pleasure, eternity and change; it subdues to union under its light yoke all irreconcilable things. It transmutes all that it touches, and every form moving within the radiance of its presence is changed by wondrous sympathy to an incarnation of the spirit which it breathes; its secret alchemy turns to potable[2] gold the poisonous waters which flow from death through life; it strips the veil of familiarity from the world, and lays bare the naked and sleeping beauty which is the spirit of its forms.

All things exist as they are perceived: at least in relation to the percipient. "The mind is its own place, and of itself can make a heaven of hell, a hell of heaven."[3] But poetry defeats the curse which binds us to be subjected to the accident of surrounding impressions. And whether it spreads its own figured curtain or withdraws life's dark veil from before the scene of things, it equally creates for us a being within our being. It makes us the inhabitants of a world to which the familiar world is a chaos. It reproduces the common universe of which we are portions and percipients, and it purges from our inward sight the film of familiarity which obscures from us the wonder of our being. It compels us to feel that which we perceive, and to imagine that which we know. It creates anew the universe after it has been annihilated in our minds by the recurrence of impressions blunted by reiteration....

The first part of these remarks has related to Poetry in its elements and principles; and it has been shown, as well as the narrow limits assigned them would permit, that what is called poetry, in a restricted sense, has a common source with all other forms of order and of beauty according to which the materials of human life are susceptible of being arranged, and which is poetry in an universal sense.

The second part[4] will have for its object an application of these principles to the present state of the cultivation of Poetry, and a defence of the attempt to idealize the modern forms of manners and opinion, and compel them into a subordination to the imaginative and creative faculty. For the

---

1   *interlunations* Periods between old and new moons; periods of darkness.
2   *potable* Drinkable. Alchemists sought a liquid form of gold that, when consumed, would be the elixir of life.
3   *The mind ... heaven* From Satan's speech in Milton's *Paradise Lost* 1.254–55.
4   *The second part* Shelley did not complete a second part.

literature of England, an energetic development of which has ever preceded or accompanied a great and free development of the national will, has arisen as it were from a new birth. In spite of the low-thoughted envy which would undervalue contemporary merit, our own will be a memorable age in intellectual achievements, and we live among such philosophers and poets as surpass beyond comparison any who have appeared since the last national struggle for civil and religious liberty.[1] The most unfailing herald, companion, and follower of the awakening of a great people to work a beneficial change in opinion or institution, is Poetry. At such periods there is an accumulation of the power of communicating and receiving intense and impassioned conceptions respecting man and nature. The persons in whom this power resides, may often, as far as regards many portions of their nature, have little apparent correspondence with that spirit of good of which they are the ministers. But even whilst they deny and abjure, they are yet compelled to serve the Power which is seated upon the throne of their own soul. It is impossible to read the compositions of the most celebrated writers of the present day without being startled with the electric life which burns within their words. They measure the circumference and sound the depths of human nature with a comprehensive and all-penetrating spirit, and they are themselves perhaps the most sincerely astonished at its manifestations, for it is less their spirit than the spirit of the age. Poets are the hierophants[2] of an unapprehended inspiration, the mirrors of the gigantic shadows which futurity casts upon the present, the words which express what they understand not; the trumpets which sing to battle, and feel not what they inspire: the influence which is moved not, but moves.[3] Poets are the unacknowledged legislators of the World.

—1820

---

1   *the last ... liberty* I.e., the English Civil War of the 1640s.
2   *hierophants* Interpreters of sacred mysteries.
3   *is moved ... moves* Reference to Greek philosopher Aristotle's description of God as the "Unmoved Mover" of the universe.

Mark Twain (Samuel Clemens)
1835–1910

Samuel Clemens spent his childhood on the banks of the Mississippi River. His pen name comes from a term used on the Mississippi to refer to the second mark on the line that measured the depth of the water—mark twain, or the two-fathom mark, was a safe depth for steamboats. His childhood adventures and life on the river also provided the background for his most popular and enduring works.

After a chequered career that included stints as a printer's apprentice, steamboat pilot, soldier, miner, and provisional governor of the territory of Nevada, Clemens began to write as "Mark Twain." His reputation as a humourist grew as he gave public lectures and published articles, travel letters, and his first book of tales, *The Celebrated Jumping Frog of Calaveras County, and other Sketches* (1867). His fame was established when an assignment to travel to Europe and the Middle East resulted in the irreverent and witty *The Innocents Abroad* (1869).

After his marriage, Twain settled down and wrote prolifically for the rest of his life, although he also undertook tours to give humourous and satirical lectures, such as "Advice to Youth" (1882). He set two novels, *The Prince and the Pauper* (1882) and *A Connecticut Yankee in King Arthur's Court* (1889), in England, but is best known for the two novels set in Twain's home state of Missouri: *The Adventures of Tom Sawyer* (1876) and *The Adventures of Huckleberry Finn* (1884). Ernest Hemingway famously said, "All modern American literature comes from one book by Mark Twain called *Huckleberry Finn*." Despite such critical admiration, this book has often generated controversy—as may be inevitable for any work that attempts to deal directly with issues of race and slavery in America.

Twain's writing continues to be highly regarded for its wit and satire, its lively depictions of Western life, and its effective use of vernacular language.

Advice to Youth

Being told I would be expected to talk here, I inquired what sort of talk I ought to make. They said it should be something suitable to youth—something didactic, instructive, or something in the nature of good advice. Very well. I have a few things in my mind which I have often longed to say for the instruction of the young; for it is in one's tender early years that such things will best take root and be most enduring and most valuable. First, then, I will say to you, my young friends—and I say it beseechingly, urgingly—

Always obey your parents, when they are present. This is the best policy in the long run, because if you don't they will make you. Most parents think they know better than you do, and you can generally make more by humouring that superstition than you can by acting on your own better judgment.

Be respectful to your superiors, if you have any, also to strangers, and sometimes to others. If a person offend you, and you are in doubt as to whether it was intentional or not, do not resort to extreme measures; simply watch your chance and hit him with a brick. That will be sufficient. If you shall find that he had not intended any offence, come out frankly and confess yourself in the wrong when you struck him; acknowledge it like a man and say you didn't mean to. Yes, always avoid violence; in this age of charity and kindliness, the time has gone by for such things. Leave dynamite to the low and unrefined.

Go to bed early, get up early—this is wise. Some authorities say get up with the sun; some others say get up with one thing, some with another. But a lark is really the best thing to get up with. It gives you a splendid reputation with everybody to know that you get up with the lark; and if you get the right kind of lark, and work at him right, you can easily train him to get up at half past nine, every time—it is no trick at all.

Now as to the matter of lying. You want to be very careful about lying; otherwise you are nearly sure to get caught. Once caught, you can never again be, in the eyes to the good and the pure, what you were before. Many a young person has injured himself permanently through a single clumsy and ill-finished lie, the result of carelessness born of incomplete training. Some authorities hold that the young ought not to lie at all. That, of course, is putting it rather stronger than necessary; still, while I cannot go quite so far as that, I do maintain, and I believe I am right, that the young ought to be temperate in the use of this great art until practice and experience shall give them that confidence, elegance, and precision which alone can make the accomplishment graceful and profitable. Patience, diligence, painstaking attention to detail—these are requirements; these, in time, will make the student perfect; upon these, and upon these only, may he rely as the sure foundation for future eminence. Think what tedious years of study, thought, practice, experience, went to the equipment of that peerless old master who was able to impose upon the whole world the lofty and sounding maxim that "truth is mighty and will prevail"—the most majestic compound fracture of fact which any of woman born has yet achieved. For the history of our race, and each individual's experience, are sown thick with evidence that a truth is not hard to kill and that a lie told well is immortal. There in Boston is a monument of the man who discovered anaesthesia;[1] many people are aware, in these latter days, that that man didn't discover it at all, but stole the discovery from another man. Is this truth mighty, and will it prevail? Ah no, my hearers, the monument is made of hardy material, but the lie it tells will outlast it a million years. An awkward, feeble, leaky lie is a thing which you ought to make it your unceasing study to avoid; such a lie as that has no more real permanence than an average truth. Why, you might as well tell the truth at once and be done with it. A feeble, stupid, preposterous lie will not live two years—except it be a slander upon somebody. It is indestructible, then, of course, but that is no merit of yours. A final word: begin your practice of this gracious and beautiful art early—begin now. If I had begun earlier, I could have learned how.

Never handle firearms carelessly. The sorrow and suffering that have been caused through the innocent but heedless handling of firearms by the young! Only four days ago, right in the next farm house to the one where I am spending the summer, a grandmother, old and grey and sweet, one of the loveliest spirits in the land, was sitting at her work, when her young grandson crept in and got down an old, battered, rusty gun which had not been touched for many years and was supposed not to be loaded, and pointed it at her, laughing and threatening to shoot. In her fright she ran screaming and pleading toward the door on the other side of the room; but as she passed him he placed the gun almost against her very breast and pulled the trigger! He had supposed it was not loaded. And he was right—it wasn't. So there wasn't any harm done. It is the only case of that kind I ever heard of. Therefore, just the same, don't you meddle with old unloaded firearms; they are the most deadly and unerring things that have ever been created by man. You don't have to take any pains at all with them; you don't have to have a rest, you don't have to have any sights on the gun, you don't have to take aim, even. No, you just pick out a relative and bang away, and you are sure to get him. A youth who can't hit a cathedral at thirty yards with a Gatling gun[2] in three quarters of an hour, can take up an old empty musket and bag his grandmother every time, at a hundred. Think what Waterloo would have been if one of the armies had been boys armed with old muskets supposed not to be loaded, and the other army had been composed of their female relations. The very thought of it makes one shudder.

---

1   *monument ... anaesthesia* Monument commemorating the work of Dr. William Thomas Green Morton (1815–68), who was the first to publicly demonstrate the use of ether as an anaesthetic. His claim to be the sole discoverer of ether's anaesthetic effects was disputed by several people.

2   *Gatling gun* Early machine gun invented in the 1860s and used by the American military.

There are many sorts of books; but good ones are the sort for the young to read. Remember that. They are a great, an inestimable, an unspeakable means of improvement. Therefore be careful in your selection, my young friends; be very careful; confine yourselves exclusively to Robertson's Sermons, Baxter's *Saint's Rest*,[1] *The Innocents Abroad*, and works of that kind.

But I have said enough. I hope you will treasure up the instructions which I have given you, and make them a guide to your feet and a light to your understanding. Build your character thoughtfully and painstaking upon these precepts, and by and by, when you have got it built, you will be surprised and gratified to see how nicely and sharply it resembles everybody else's.

—(1882)

---

1   *Robertson's Sermons* Sermons by Anglican minister F.W. Robertson (1816–53), which were published in the decade after his death and were widely read and respected; *Baxter's Saint's Rest* Richard Baxter's devotional work *The Saint's Everlasting Rest* (1650), considered a spiritual classic.

Virginia Woolf
1882–1941

As a writer of daring and ambitious novels; a publisher of avant-garde work by figures such as T.S. Eliot and Katherine Mansfield; and a founding member of the Bloomsbury Group, a circle of brilliant English artists and intellectuals, Virginia Woolf was at the forefront of literary modernism and its revolt against traditional forms and styles. Today, she is admired and studied primarily as the author of such masterpieces as *Mrs Dalloway* (1925), *To the Lighthouse* (1927), and *The Waves* (1931), novels that attempt to capture the rhythms of consciousness by rendering the subjective interplay of perception, recollection, emotion, and understanding. But in her own lifetime Woolf was just as well known for her non-fiction, a vast body of journalism, criticism, and essays in which she draws on "the democratic art of prose" (in her own words) to communicate with a broader readership.

Two of Woolf's longer non-fiction works, *A Room of One's Own* (1929) and *Three Guineas* (1938), are now acknowledged as ground-breaking feminist studies of the social, psychological, and political effects of patriarchy. But many critics have tended to treat Woolf's essays as incidental works, interesting only insofar as they illuminate her fictional theory and practice. Woolf herself distinguished between professional and creative writing—the one a means to an income, the other part of a broader artistic project. The essays tend to be more formally conventional than the novels, but many of them are nonetheless remarkable for their expression of personality and their open engagement with ideas. Amiable and urbane, more exploratory than authoritative, they wander from topic to topic, full of idiosyncratic asides and digressions. Through her engagingly forthright tone Woolf often achieves a remarkable intimacy with the reader. She considered the possibility for creating such intimacy to be a chief virtue of the form: as she observed, a good essay "must draw its curtain round us, but it must be a curtain that shuts us in, not out."

The Death of the Moth

Moths that fly by day are not properly to be called moths; they do not excite that pleasant sense of dark autumn nights and ivy-blossom which the commonest yellow-underwing asleep in the shadow of the curtain never fails to rouse in us. They are hybrid creatures, neither gay like butterflies nor sombre like their own species. Nevertheless the present specimen, with his narrow hay-coloured wings, fringed with a tassel of the same colour, seemed to be content with life. It was a pleasant morning, mid–September, mild, benignant, yet with a keener breath than that of the summer months. The plough was already scoring the field opposite the window, and where the share[1] had been, the earth was pressed flat and gleamed with moisture. Such vigour came rolling in from the fields and the down beyond that it was difficult to keep the eyes strictly turned upon the book. The rooks too were keeping one of their annual festivities; soaring round the tree tops until it looked as if a vast net with thousands of black knots in it had been cast up into the air; which, after a few moments sank slowly down upon the trees until every twig seemed to have a knot at the end of it. Then, suddenly, the net would be thrown into the air again in a wider circle this time, with the utmost clamour and vociferation, as though to be thrown into the air and settle slowly down upon the tree tops were a tremendously exciting experience.

The same energy which inspired the rooks, the ploughmen, the horses, and even, it seemed, the lean bare-backed downs, sent the moth fluttering from side to side of his square of the window-pane. One could not help watching him. One was, indeed, conscious of a queer feeling of pity for him. The possibilities of pleasure seemed that morning so enormous and so various that to have only a moth's part in life, and a day moth's at that, appeared a hard fate, and his zest in enjoying his meagre opportunities to the full, pathetic. He flew vigorously to one corner of his compartment, and, after waiting there a second, flew across to the other. What remained for him but to fly to a third corner and then to a fourth? That was all he could do, in spite of the size of the downs, the width of the sky, the far-off smoke of houses, and the romantic voice, now and then, of a steamer out at sea. What he could do he did. Watching him, it seemed as if a fibre, very thin but pure, of the enormous energy of the world had been thrust into his frail and diminutive body. As often as he crossed the pane, I could fancy that a thread of vital light became visible. He was little or nothing but life.

Yet, because he was so small, and so simple a form of the energy that was rolling in at the open window and driving its way through so many narrow and intricate corridors in my own brain and in those of other human beings, there was something marvellous as well as pathetic about him. It was as if someone had taken a tiny bead of pure life and decking it as lightly as possible with down and feathers, had set it dancing and zig-zagging to show us the true nature of life. Thus displayed one could not get over the strangeness of it. One is apt to forget all about life, seeing it humped and bossed and garnished and cumbered so that it has to move with the greatest circumspection and dignity. Again, the thought of all that life might have been had he been born in any other shape caused one to view his simple activities with a kind of pity.

---

1   *share* Blade of a plough.

After a time, tired by his dancing apparently, he settled on the window ledge in the sun, and, the queer spectacle being at an end, I forgot about him. Then, looking up, my eye was caught by him. He was trying to resume his dancing, but seemed either so stiff or so awkward that he could only flutter to the bottom of the window-pane; and when he tried to fly across it he failed. Being intent on other matters I watched these futile attempts for a time without thinking, unconsciously waiting for him to resume his flight, as one waits for a machine, that has stopped momentarily, to start again without considering the reason of its failure. After perhaps a seventh attempt he slipped from the wooden ledge and fell, fluttering his wings, on to his back on the window sill. The helplessness of his attitude roused me. It flashed upon me that he was in difficulties; he could no longer raise himself; his legs struggled vainly. But, as I stretched out a pencil, meaning to help him to right himself, it came over me that the failure and awkwardness were the approach of death. I laid the pencil down again.

The legs agitated themselves once more. I looked as if for the enemy against which he struggled. I looked out of doors. What had happened there? Presumably it was midday, and work in the fields had stopped. Stillness and quiet had replaced the previous animation. The birds had taken themselves off to feed in the brooks. The horses stood still. Yet the power was there all the same, massed outside indifferent, impersonal, not attending to anything in particular. Somehow it was opposed to the little hay-coloured moth. It was useless to try to do anything. One could only watch the extraordinary efforts made by those tiny legs against an oncoming doom which could, had it chosen, have submerged an entire city, not merely a city, but masses of human beings; nothing, I knew, had any chance against death. Nevertheless after a pause of exhaustion the legs fluttered again. It was superb this last protest, and so frantic that he succeeded at last in righting himself. One's sympathies, of course, were all on the side of life. Also, when there was nobody to care or to know, this gigantic effort on the part of an insignificant little moth, against a power of such magnitude, to retain what no one else valued or desired to keep, moved one strangely. Again, somehow, one saw life, a pure bead. I lifted the pencil again, useless though I knew it to be. But even as I did so, the unmistakable tokens of death showed themselves. The body relaxed, and instantly grew stiff. The struggle was over. The insignificant little creature now knew death. As I looked at the dead moth, this minute wayside triumph of so great a force over so mean an antagonist filled me with wonder. Just as life had been strange a few minutes before, so death was now as strange. The moth having righted himself now lay most decently and uncomplainingly composed. O yes, he seemed to say, death is stronger than I am.

—1942

Zora Neale Hurston

1891–1960

Today critics often speak of the resurrection of Zora Neale Hurston. Although among the most prolific African American writers of her generation, she spent her latter years in obscurity, earning a paltry and irregular subsistence as a maid, supply teacher, and sometime journalist. When she died in a county welfare home in Florida, she was buried in an unmarked grave, her achievements largely ignored or forgotten. It was not until 1975, when Alice Walker published her essay "In Search of Zora Neale Hurston," that the author of *Jonah's Gourd Vine* (1934) and *Their Eyes Were Watching God* (1937) was restored to her rightful place and recognized as "the intellectual and spiritual foremother of a generation of black women writers."

Many commentators on Hurston's novels, short stories, and pioneering studies of African folklore have been struck by what Walker describes as their exuberant "racial health—a sense of black people as complete, complex, *undiminished* human beings, a sense that is lacking in so much black writing and literature." Informed by the myths, rituals, and storytelling traditions that she documented in her anthropological work, Hurston's fiction celebrates black culture and the nuance and vitality of black vernacular speech. But her reluctance to use her art to "lecture on the race problem" or to give a politicized, sociological account of "the Negro" alienated many other prominent authors and intellectuals of the Harlem Renaissance. In a rancorous review of *Their Eyes Were Watching God*, Richard Wright accused Hurston of perpetuating a degrading minstrel tradition, dismissing her masterpiece as an exercise in "facile sensuality" that "carries no theme, no message, no thought."

Ever an individualist, Hurston refused to write resentful novels of social protest in which "black lives are only defensive reactions to white actions." As she declared in her essay "How It Feels to Be Coloured Me" (1928), "I do not belong to that sobbing school of Negrohood who hold that nature somehow has given them a lowdown dirty deal." Hurston's position was controversial, particularly in the era of Jim Crow segregation laws, but she sought after her own fashion to overcome what W.E.B. Du Bois called "the problem of the color line" by opening up the souls of black men and women so as to reveal their common humanity and individual strength.

How It Feels to Be Coloured Me

I am coloured but I offer nothing in the way of extenuating circumstances except the fact that I am the only Negro in the United States whose grandfather on the mother's side was *not* an Indian chief.[1]

I remember the very day that I became coloured. Up to my thirteenth year I lived in the little Negro town of Eatonville, Florida. It is exclusively a coloured town. The only white people I knew passed through the town going to or coming from Orlando. The native whites rode dusty horses, the Northern tourists chugged down the sandy village road in automobiles. The town knew the Southerners and never stopped cane chewing when they passed. But the Northerners were something else again. They were peered at cautiously from behind curtains by the timid. The more venturesome would come out on the porch to watch them go past and got just as much pleasure out of the tourists as the tourists got out of the village.

The front porch might seem a daring place for the rest of the town, but it was a gallery[2] seat for me. My favourite place was atop the gate-post. Proscenium box for a born first-nighter.[3] Not only did I enjoy the show, but I didn't mind the actors knowing that I liked it. I usually spoke to them in passing. I'd wave at them and when they returned my salute, I would say something like this: "Howdy-do-well-I-thank-you-where-you-goin'?" Usually the automobile or the horse paused at this, and after a queer exchange of compliments, I would probably "go a piece of the way" with them, as we say in farthest Florida. If one of my family happened to come to the front in time to see me, of course negotiations would be rudely broken off. But even so, it is clear that I was the first "welcome-to-our-state" Floridian, and I hope the Miami Chamber of Commerce will please take notice.

During this period, white people differed from coloured to me only in that they rode through town and never lived there. They liked to hear me "speak pieces" and sing and wanted to see me dance the parse-me-la, and gave me generously of their small silver for doing these things, which seemed strange to me for I wanted to do them so much that I needed bribing to stop. Only they didn't know it. The coloured people gave no dimes. They deplored any joyful tendencies in me, but I was their Zora nevertheless. I belonged to them, to the nearby hotels, to the county—everybody's Zora.

---

1   *I am … Indian chief* An improbably high number of African Americans claimed to have Native American heritage, which was prestigious in African American communities at this time.

2   *gallery* Theatre seating area situated in an elevated balcony.

3   *Proscenium box* Theatre seating area near the proscenium, the frame of the stage; *first-nighter* Person who frequently appears in the audience of opening night performances.

But changes came in the family when I was thirteen, and I was sent to school in Jacksonville. I left Eatonville, the town of the oleanders, as Zora. When I disembarked from the river-boat at Jacksonville, she was no more. It seemed that I had suffered a sea change. I was not Zora of Orange County any more, I was now a little coloured girl. I found it out in certain ways. In my heart as well as in the mirror, I became a fast[1] brown—warranted not to rub nor run.

But I am not tragically coloured. There is no great sorrow dammed up in my soul, nor lurking behind my eyes. I do not mind at all. I do not belong to the sobbing school of Negrohood who hold that nature somehow has given them a lowdown dirty deal and whose feelings are all hurt about it. Even in the helter-skelter skirmish that is my life, I have seen that the world is to the strong regardless of a little pigmentation more or less. No, I do not weep at the world—I am too busy sharpening my oyster knife.

Someone is always at my elbow reminding me that I am the granddaughter of slaves. It fails to register depression with me. Slavery is sixty years in the past.[2] The operation was successful and the patient is doing well, thank you. The terrible struggle that made me an American out of a potential slave said "On the line!" The Reconstruction[3] said "Get set!"; and the generation before said "Go!" I am off to a flying start and I must not halt in the stretch to look behind and weep. Slavery is the price I paid for civilization, and the choice was not with me. It is a bully[4] adventure and worth all that I have paid through my ancestors for it. No one on earth ever had a greater chance for glory. The world to be won and nothing to be lost. It is thrilling to think—to know that for any act of mine, I shall get twice as much praise or twice as much blame. It is quite exciting to hold the centre of the national stage, with the spectators not knowing whether to laugh or to weep.

The position of my white neighbour is much more difficult. No brown spectre pulls up a chair beside me when I sit down to eat. No dark ghost thrusts its leg against mine in bed. The game of keeping what one has is never so exciting as the game of getting.

---

1   *fast* Adjective applied to dyes that will not run or change colour.

2   *Slavery is … the past* In 1863, the Emancipation Proclamation legally ended slavery in America.

3   *Reconstruction* Period of recovery (1865–77) after the American Civil War. During Reconstruction, the Southern states adjusted to an economy without legal slavery and rebuilt infrastructure that had been damaged by the war.

4   *bully* Merry, splendid.

I do not always feel coloured. Even now I often achieve the unconscious Zora of Eatonville before the Hegira.[1] I feel most coloured when I am thrown against a sharp white background.

For instance at Barnard.[2] "Beside the waters of the Hudson"[3] I feel my race. Among the thousand white persons, I am a dark rock surged upon, and overswept, but through it all, I remain myself. When covered by the waters, I am; and the ebb but reveals me again.

Sometimes it is the other way around. A white person is set down in our midst, but the contrast is just as sharp for me. For instance, when I sit in the drafty basement that is The New World Cabaret with a white person, my colour comes. We enter chatting about any little nothing that we have in common and are seated by the jazz waiters. In the abrupt way that jazz orchestras have, this one plunges into a number. It loses no time in circumlocutions, but gets right down to business. It constricts the thorax and splits the heart with its tempo and narcotic harmonies. This orchestra grows rambunctious, rears on its hind legs and attacks the tonal veil with primitive fury, rending it, clawing it until it breaks through to the jungle beyond. I follow those heathen—follow them exultingly. I dance wildly inside myself; I yell within, I whoop; I shake my assegai[4] above my head, I hurl it true to the mark *yeeeeooww*! I am in the jungle and living in the jungle way. My face is painted red and yellow and my body is painted blue. My pulse is throbbing like a war drum. I want to slaughter something—give pain, give death to what, I do not know. But the piece ends. The men of the orchestra wipe their lips and rest their fingers. I creep back slowly to the veneer we call civilization with the last tone and find the white friend sitting motionless in his seat smoking calmly.

"Good music they have here," he remarks, drumming the table with his fingertips.

Music. The great blobs of purple and red emotion have not touched him. He has only heard what I felt. He is far away and I see him but dimly across the ocean and the continent that have fallen between us. He is so pale with his whiteness then and I am *so* coloured.

At certain times I have no race, I am *me*. When I set my hat at a certain angle and saunter down Seventh Avenue, Harlem City, feeling as snooty as the lions

---

1   *Hegira* I.e., journey; refers to Mohammed's journey from Mecca to Medina, which marks the beginning of the current era in the Islamic calendar.

2   *Barnard* Women's liberal arts college in New York City, affiliated with Columbia University.

3   *Beside ... Hudson* Barnard school song.

4   *assegai* Spear made of a tree of the same name, used by people of southern Africa.

in front of the Forty-Second Street Library, for instance. So far as my feelings are concerned, Peggy Hopkins Joyce on the Boule Mich[1] with her gorgeous raiment, stately carriage, knees knocking together in a most aristocratic manner, has nothing on me. The cosmic Zora emerges. I belong to no race nor time. I am the eternal feminine with its string of beads.

I have no separate feeling about being an American citizen and coloured. I am merely a fragment of the Great Soul that surges within the boundaries. My country, right or wrong.

Sometimes, I feel discriminated against, but it does not make me angry. It merely astonishes me. How *can* any deny themselves the pleasure of my company? It's beyond me.

But in the main, I feel like a brown bag of miscellany propped against a wall. Against a wall in company with other bags, white, red and yellow. Pour out the contents, and there is discovered a jumble of small things priceless and worthless. A first-water[2] diamond, an empty spool, bits of broken glass, lengths of string, a key to a door long since crumbled away, a rusty knife-blade, old shoes saved for a road that never was and never will be, a nail bent under the weight of things too heavy for any nail, a dried flower or two still a little fragrant. In your hand is the brown bag. On the ground before you is the jumble it held—so much like the jumble in the bags, could they be emptied, that all might be dumped in a single heap and the bags refilled without altering the content of any greatly. A bit of coloured glass more or less would not matter. Perhaps that is how the Great Stuffer of Bags filled them in the first place—who knows?

—1928

---

1   *Peggy Hopkins Joyce* White American actress (1893–1957) known for her extravagant lifestyle; *Boule Mich* Boulevard Saint-Michel, a major street in Paris.

2   *first-water* Best quality of diamond or other gem.

rge Orwell

)50

George Orwell is best known to modern readers for two works: the anti-Stalinist allegory *Animal Farm* (1945) and the dystopian nightmare *1984* (1949). It was with reference to these two novels that the word "Orwellian" entered the English language as a signifier for any oppressive, invasive, and manipulative practice that seems to threaten the freedom of a society. Orwell was also a successful and prolific writer of non-fiction: full-length works of political and social criticism (notably *The Road to Wigan Pier*, *Down and Out in Paris and London*, and *Homage to Catalonia*) as well as essays of a variety of sorts (memoir, literary criticism, political journalism). The imprint he left on English literary non-fiction may be even deeper than that which he left on English fiction; the scholar Leo Rockas has said that "Orwell's style is probably more admired and pointed to as a model than any other modern prose style, primarily for its no-nonsense approach."

Eric Arthur Blair, the man who would become famous as George Orwell, was born in the Indian municipality of Motihari to an English father employed in the Indian Civil Service. His mother had grown up in Burma, where her French father pursued his business interests. When he was one year old, his mother took him and his older sister to live in England; there, Orwell attended a number of boarding schools, including Eton, in preparation for a university career. His Eastern origins, however, exerted a strong influence on the young man, and in 1922 Orwell left England to begin service with the Indian Imperial Police in Burma.

Orwell's time in Burma would inform his art and politics for the rest of his life. Most directly, he would draw on his experiences in writing essays such as "Shooting an Elephant" (1936). Beyond that, the distaste he developed in Burma for the imperial project continued to inform Orwell's treatment of the themes of authority, oppression, and moral conscience—in the novels *Animal Farm* and *1984* as well as in his non-fiction.

Shooting an Elephant

In Moulmein, in Lower Burma, I was hated by large numbers of people—the only time in my life that I have been important enough for this to happen to me. I was sub-divisional police officer of the town, and in an aimless, petty kind of way anti-European feeling was very bitter. No one had the guts to raise a riot, but if a European woman went through the bazaars alone somebody would probably spit betel[1] juice over her dress. As a police officer I was an ob-

---

1   *betel* Leaf and nut mixture that is chewed as a stimulant, common in Southeast Asia.

vious target and was baited whenever it seemed safe to do so. When a nimble
Burman tripped me up on the football field and the referee (another Burman)
looked the other way, the crowd yelled with hideous laughter. This happened
more than once. In the end the sneering yellow faces of young men that met
me everywhere, the insults hooted after me when I was at a safe distance, got
badly on my nerves. The young Buddhist priests were the worst of all. There
were several thousands of them in the town and none of them seemed to have
anything to do except stand on street corners and jeer at Europeans.

All this was perplexing and upsetting. For at that time I had already made
up my mind that imperialism was an evil thing and the sooner I chucked up
my job and got out of it the better. Theoretically—and secretly, of course—I
was all for the Burmese and all against their oppressors, the British. As for the
job I was doing, I hated it more bitterly than I can perhaps make clear. In a job
like that you see the dirty work of Empire at close quarters. The wretched prisoners huddling in the stinking cages of the lock-ups, the grey, cowed faces of
the long-term convicts, the scarred buttocks of the men who had been flogged
with bamboos—all these oppressed me with an intolerable sense of guilt. But
I could get nothing into perspective. I was young and ill-educated and I had
had to think out my problems in the utter silence that is imposed on every
Englishman in the East. I did not even know that the British Empire is dying,
still less did I know that it is a great deal better than the younger empires that
are going to supplant it. All I knew was that I was stuck between my hatred
of the empire I served and my rage against the evil-spirited little beasts who
tried to make my job impossible. With one part of my mind I thought of the
British Raj as an unbreakable tyranny, as something clamped down, *in saecula
saeculorum*,[1] upon the will of prostrate peoples; with another part I thought
that the greatest joy in the world would be to drive a bayonet into a Buddhist
priest's guts. Feelings like these are the normal by-products of imperialism; ask
any Anglo-Indian official, if you can catch him off duty.

One day something happened which in a roundabout way was enlighten-
ing. It was a tiny incident in itself, but it gave me a better glimpse than I had
had before of the real nature of imperialism—the real motives for which des-
potic governments act. Early one morning the sub-inspector at a police station
the other end of the town rang me up on the phone and said that an elephant
was ravaging the bazaar. Would I please come and do something about it? I
did not know what I could do, but I wanted to see what was happening and I
got on to a pony and started out. I took my rifle, an old .44 Winchester and
much too small to kill an elephant, but I thought the noise might be useful *in*

---

1   *in saecula saeculorum* Latin: for centuries upon centuries; forever. This phrase appears
frequently in the New Testament.

terrorem.[1] Various Burmans stopped me on the way and told me about the elephant's doings. It was not, of course, a wild elephant, but a tame one which had gone "must."[2] It had been chained up, as tame elephants always are when their attack of "must" is due, but on the previous night it had broken its chain and escaped. Its mahout,[3] the only person who could manage it when it was in that state, had set out in pursuit, but had taken the wrong direction and was now twelve hours' journey away, and in the morning the elephant had suddenly reappeared in the town. The Burmese population had no weapons and were quite helpless against it. It had already destroyed somebody's bamboo hut, killed a cow and raided some fruit-stalls and devoured the stock; also it had met the municipal rubbish van and, when the driver jumped out and took to his heels, had turned the van over and inflicted violences upon it.

The Burmese sub-inspector and some Indian constables were waiting for me in the quarter where the elephant had been seen. It was a very poor quarter, a labyrinth of squalid bamboo huts, thatched with palmleaf, winding all over a steep hillside. I remember that it was a cloudy, stuffy morning at the beginning of the rains. We began questioning the people as to where the elephant had gone and, as usual, failed to get any definite information. That is invariably the case in the East; a story always sounds clear enough at a distance, but the nearer you get to the scene of events the vaguer it becomes. Some of the people said that the elephant had gone in one direction, some said that he had gone in another, some professed not even to have heard of any elephant. I had almost made up my mind that the whole story was a pack of lies, when we heard yells a little distance away. There was a loud, scandalized cry of "Go away, child! Go away this instant!" and an old woman with a switch in her hand came round the corner of a hut, violently shooing away a crowd of naked children. Some more women followed, clicking their tongues and exclaiming; evidently there was something that the children ought not to have seen. I rounded the hut and saw a man's dead body sprawling in the mud. He was an Indian, a black Dravidian coolie,[4] almost naked, and he could not have been dead many minutes. The people said that the elephant had come suddenly upon him round the corner of the hut, caught him with its trunk, put its foot on his back and ground him into the earth. This was the rainy season and the ground was soft, and his face had scored a trench a foot deep and a couple of yards long. He was lying on his belly with arms crucified and head sharply twisted to one side. His face was coated with mud, the eyes wide open, the

---

1   *in terrorem* Legal term for a warning; literally, Latin phrase meaning "in fear or alarm."
2   *must* Condition characterized by aggressive behaviour brought on by a surge in testosterone.
3   *mahout* Elephant trainer or keeper.
4   *Dravidian coolie* I.e., southern Indian manual labourer.

teeth bared and grinning with an expression of unendurable agony. (Never tell me, by the way, that the dead look peaceful. Most of the corpses I have seen looked devilish.) The friction of the great beast's foot had stripped the skin from his back as neatly as one skins a rabbit. As soon as I saw the dead man I sent an orderly to a friend's house nearby to borrow an elephant rifle. I had already sent back the pony, not wanting it to go mad with fright and throw me if it smelt the elephant.

The orderly came back in a few minutes with a rifle and five cartridges, and meanwhile some Burmans had arrived and told us that the elephant was in the paddy fields below, only a few hundred yards away. As I started forward practically the whole population of the quarter flocked out of the houses and followed me. They had seen the rifle and were all shouting excitedly that I was going to shoot the elephant. They had not shown much interest in the elephant when he was merely ravaging their homes, but it was different now that he was going to be shot. It was a bit of fun to them, as it would be to an English crowd; besides they wanted the meat. It made me vaguely uneasy. I had no intention of shooting the elephant—I had merely sent for the rifle to defend myself if necessary—and it is always unnerving to have a crowd following you. I marched down the hill, looking and feeling a fool, with the rifle over my shoulder and an ever-growing army of people jostling at my heels. At the bottom, when you got away from the huts, there was a metalled road and beyond that a miry waste of paddy fields a thousand yards across, not yet ploughed but soggy from the first rains and dotted with coarse grass. The elephant was standing eight yards from the road, his left side towards us. He took not the slightest notice of the crowd's approach. He was tearing up bunches of grass, beating them against his knees to clean them and stuffing them into his mouth.

I had halted on the road. As soon as I saw the elephant I knew with perfect certainty that I ought not to shoot him. It is a serious matter to shoot a working elephant—it is comparable to destroying a huge and costly piece of machinery—and obviously one ought not to do it if it can possibly be avoided. And at that distance, peacefully eating, the elephant looked no more dangerous than a cow. I thought then and I think now that his attack of 'must' was already passing off; in which case he would merely wander harmlessly about until the mahout came back and caught him. Moreover, I did not in the least want to shoot him. I decided that I would watch him for a little while to make sure that he did not turn savage again, and then go home.

But at that moment I glanced round at the crowd that had followed me. It was an immense crowd, two thousand at the least and growing every minute. It blocked the road for a long distance on either side. I looked at the sea of yellow faces above the garish clothes—faces all happy and excited over this bit of fun, all certain that the elephant was going to be shot. They were watching me as they would watch a conjurer about to perform a trick. They did not like me, but with the magical rifle in my hands I was momentarily worth watching. And suddenly I realized that I should have to shoot the elephant after all. The people expected it of me and I had got to do it; I could feel their two thousand wills pressing me forward, irresistibly. And it was at this moment, as I stood there with the rifle in my hands, that I first grasped the hollowness, the futility of the white man's dominion in the East. Here was I, the white man with his gun, standing in front of the unarmed native crowd—seemingly the leading actor of the piece; but in reality I was only an absurd puppet pushed to and fro by the will of those yellow faces behind. I perceived in this moment that when the white man turns tyrant it is his own freedom that he destroys. He becomes a sort of hollow, posing dummy, the conventionalized figure of a sahib.[1] For it is the condition of his rule that he shall spend his life in trying to impress the "natives," and so in every crisis he has got to do what the "natives" expect of him. He wears a mask, and his face grows to fit it. I had got to shoot the elephant. I had committed myself to doing it when I sent for the rifle. A sahib has got to act like a sahib; he has got to appear resolute, to know his own mind and do definite things. To come all that way, rifle in hand, with two thousand people marching at my heels, and then to trail feebly away, having done nothing—no, that was impossible. The crowd would laugh at me. And my whole life, every white man's life in the East, was one long struggle not to be laughed at.

But I did not want to shoot the elephant. I watched him beating his bunch of grass against his knees, with that preoccupied grandmotherly air that elephants have. It seemed to me that it would be murder to shoot him. At that age I was not squeamish about killing animals, but I had never shot an elephant and never wanted to. (Somehow it always seems worse to kill a *large* animal.) Besides, there was the beast's owner to be considered. Alive, the elephant was worth at least a hundred pounds; dead, he would only be worth the value of his tusks, five pounds, possibly. But I had got to act quickly. I turned to some experienced-looking Burmans who had been there when we arrived, and asked them how the elephant had been behaving. They all said the same thing: he took no notice of you if you left him alone, but he might charge if you went too close to him.

It was perfectly clear to me what I ought to do. I ought to walk up to within, say, twenty-five yards of the elephant and test his behaviour. If he charged, I could shoot; if he took no notice of me, it would be safe to leave

---

1   *sahib* I.e., colonial Englishman; this title of respect was used to address European men in colonial India.

him until the mahout came back. But also I knew that I was going to do no such thing. I was a poor shot with a rifle and the ground was soft mud into which one would sink at every step. If the elephant charged and I missed him, I should have about as much chance as a toad under a steam-roller. But even then I was not thinking particularly of my own skin, only of the watchful yellow faces behind. For at that moment, with the crowd watching me, I was not afraid in the ordinary sense, as I would have been if I had been alone. A white man mustn't be frightened in front of "natives"; and so, in general, he isn't frightened. The sole thought in my mind was that if anything went wrong those two thousand Burmans would see me pursued, caught, trampled on and reduced to a grinning corpse like that Indian up the hill. And if that happened it was quite probable that some of them would laugh. That would never do.

There was only one alternative. I shoved the cartridges into the magazine and lay down on the road to get a better aim. The crowd grew very still, and a deep, low, happy sigh, as of people who see the theatre curtain go up at last, breathed from innumerable throats. They were going to have their bit of fun after all. The rifle was a beautiful German thing with cross-hair sights. I did not then know that in shooting an elephant one would shoot to cut an imaginary bar running from ear-hole to ear-hole. I ought, therefore, as the elephant was sideways on, to have aimed straight at his ear-hole, actually I aimed several inches in front of this, thinking the brain would be further forward.

When I pulled the trigger I did not hear the bang or feel the kick—one never does when a shot goes home—but I heard the devilish roar of glee that went up from the crowd. In that instant, in too short a time, one would have thought, even for the bullet to get there, a mysterious, terrible change had come over the elephant. He neither stirred nor fell, but every line of his body had altered. He looked suddenly stricken, shrunken, immensely old, as though the frightful impact of the bullet had paralysed him without knocking him down. At last, after what seemed a long time—it might have been five seconds, I dare say—he sagged flabbily to his knees. His mouth slobbered. An enormous senility seemed to have settled upon him. One could have imagined him thousands of years old. I fired again into the same spot. At the second shot he did not collapse but climbed with desperate slowness to his feet and stood weakly upright, with legs sagging and head drooping. I fired a third time. That was the shot that did for him. You could see the agony of it jolt his whole body and knock the last remnant of strength from his legs. But in falling he seemed for a moment to rise, for as his hind legs collapsed beneath him he seemed to tower upward like a huge rock toppling, his trunk reaching skyward like a tree. He trumpeted, for the first and only time. And then down he came, his belly towards me, with a crash that seemed to shake the ground even where I lay.

I got up. The Burmans were already racing past me across the mud. It was obvious that the elephant would never rise again, but he was not dead. He was breathing very rhythmically with long rattling gasps, his great mound of a side painfully rising and falling. His mouth was wide open—I could see far down into caverns of pale pink throat. I waited a long time for him to die, but his breathing did not weaken. Finally I fired my two remaining shots into the spot where I thought his heart must be. The thick blood welled out of him like red velvet, but still he did not die. His body did not even jerk when the shots hit him, the tortured breathing continued without a pause. He was dying, very slowly and in great agony, but in some world remote from me where not even a bullet could damage him further. I felt that I had got to put an end to that dreadful noise. It seemed dreadful to see the great beast lying there, powerless to move and yet powerless to die, and not even to be able to finish him. I sent back for my small rifle and poured shot after shot into his heart and down his throat. They seemed to make no impression. The tortured gasps continued as steadily as the ticking of a clock.

In the end I could not stand it any longer and went away. I heard later that it took him half an hour to die. Burmans were bringing dahs[1] and baskets even before I left, and I was told they had stripped his body almost to the bones by the afternoon.

Afterwards, of course, there were endless discussions about the shooting of the elephant. The owner was furious, but he was only an Indian and could do nothing. Besides, legally I had done the right thing, for a mad elephant has to be killed, like a mad dog, if its owner fails to control it. Among the Europeans opinion was divided. The older men said I was right, the younger men said it was a damn shame to shoot an elephant for killing a coolie, because an elephant was worth more than any damn Coringhee[2] coolie. And afterwards I was very glad that the coolie had been killed; it put me legally in the right and it gave me a sufficient pretext for shooting the elephant. I often wondered whether any of the others grasped that I had done it solely to avoid looking a fool.

—1936

---

1   *dahs* Short swords or knives.
2   *Coringhee* From Coringha, a town on the coast of India.

Roland Barthes
1915–1980

Although scholars continue to debate the nature of his achievement, Roland Barthes, French critic, theorist, and champion of the avant-garde, was undoubtedly among the most influential intellectuals of the twentieth century. A pioneer in the field of semiology (the science of signs), and a trenchant critic of bourgeois culture and of the attitudes and values implicit in its icons, institutions, and "myths," Barthes has himself become something of a cultural icon. He is also famous for proclaiming "the death of the author" as the sovereign authority over textual meaning. Barthes is a difficult writer with whom to come to grips; the range of his interests and his highly idiosyncratic prose seem to be continually shifting—as are the contours of his thought.

Barthes is best known for his work on structuralism, an intellectual movement that grew out of the application of the methods and principles of structural linguistics to analyses of cultural phenomena, as a means of uncovering the system of codes and conventions whereby those phenomena are understood. He was also keenly interested in what he called "unlearning," the study of what is forgotten or taken for granted. By unmasking that which goes without saying, Barthes aims to reveal how the seemingly natural, self-evident meanings that circulate within a culture are in fact cultural products that support ideologies and serve particular social interests. We see this at play in *Mythologies* (1957), where Barthes brings his analytical powers to bear on a diverse host of subjects—wrestling, film, photography, wine, even children's toys—in an effort to expose the ideologically loaded secondary messages they emit.

Barthes is not without his detractors: skeptics have dismissed him as a dilettante whose convoluted theoretical pretensions ultimately lead to an intellectual dead end. But, as a "public experimenter" who took up and tested novel ideas and methods, Barthes opened new frontiers of critical study, challenging and transforming conventional views of authorship, realism, representation, the reading process, and the relationship between text and history.

World of Wrestling

The grandiloquent truth of gestures on life's great occasions.[1]
—BAUDELAIRE

The virtue of all-in wrestling is that it is the spectacle of excess. Here we find a grandiloquence which must have been that of the ancient theatres. And in fact wrestling is an open-air spectacle, for what makes the circus[2] or the arena what they are is not the sky (a romantic value suited rather to fashionable occasions), it is the drenching and vertical quality of the flood of light. Even hidden in the most squalid Parisian halls, wrestling partakes of the nature of the great solar spectacles, Greek drama[3] and bull-fights: in both, a light without shadow generates an emotion without reserve.

There are people who think that wrestling is an ignoble sport. Wrestling is not a sport, it is a spectacle, and it is no more ignoble to attend a wrestled performance of Suffering than a performance of the sorrows of Arnolphe or Andromaque.[4] Of course, there exists a false wrestling, in which the participants unnecessarily go to great lengths to make a show of a fair fight; this is of no interest. True wrestling, wrongly called amateur wrestling, is performed in second-rate halls, where the public spontaneously attunes itself to the spectacular nature of the contest, like the audience at a suburban cinema. Then these same people wax indignant because wrestling is a stage-managed sport (which ought, by the way, to mitigate its ignominy). The public is completely uninterested in knowing whether the contest is rigged or not, and rightly so; it abandons itself to the primary virtue of the spectacle, which is to abolish all motives and all consequences: what matters is not what it thinks but what it sees.

This public knows very well the distinction between wrestling and boxing; it knows that boxing is ... based on a demonstration of excellence. One can bet on the outcome of a boxing-match: with wrestling, it would make no sense. A boxing-match is a story which is constructed before the eyes of the spectator; in wrestling, on the contrary, it is each moment which is intelligible, not the passage of time. The spectator is not interested in the rise and fall of

---

1 *The grandiloquent ... great occasions* From Charles Baudelaire, *Curiosités Esthétiques* (1868); *grandiloquent* Showy, grandiosely expressive.
2 *circus* Ancient outdoor stadium.
3 *Greek drama* In Ancient Athens, tragedies and comedies were performed in large outdoor arenas as part of mass religious festivals.
4 *Arnolphe* Protagonist of *The School for Wives* (1662), a play by the greatly admired French writer Molière; *Andromaque* Title character of a 1667 tragedy by Jean Racine, another widely respected French playwright.

fortunes; he expects the transient image of certain passions. Wrestling therefore demands an immediate reading of the juxtaposed meanings, so that there is no need to connect them. The logical conclusion of the contest does not interest the wrestling-fan, while on the contrary a boxing-match always implies a science of the future. In other words, wrestling is a sum of spectacles, of which no single one is a function: each moment imposes the total knowledge of a passion which rises erect and alone, without ever extending to the crowning moment of a result.

Thus the function of the wrestler is not to win; it is to go exactly through the motions which are expected of him. It is said that judo contains a hidden symbolic aspect; even in the midst of efficiency, its gestures are measured, precise but restricted, drawn accurately but by a stroke without volume. Wrestling, on the contrary, offers excessive gestures, exploited to the limit of their meaning. In judo, a man who is down is hardly down at all, he rolls over, he draws back, he eludes defeat, or, if the latter is obvious, he immediately disappears; in wrestling, a man who is down is exaggeratedly so, and completely fills the eyes of the spectators with the intolerable spectacle of his powerlessness.

This function of grandiloquence is indeed the same as that of ancient theatre, whose principle, language and props (masks and buskins[1]) concurred in the exaggeratedly visible explanation of a Necessity. The gesture of the vanquished wrestler signifying to the world a defeat which, far from disguising, he emphasizes and holds like a pause in music, corresponds to the mask of antiquity meant to signify the tragic mode of the spectacle. In wrestling, as on the stage in antiquity, one is not ashamed of one's suffering, one knows how to cry, one has a liking for tears.

Each sign[2] in wrestling is therefore endowed with an absolute clarity, since one must always understand everything on the spot. As soon as the adversaries are in the ring, the public is overwhelmed with the obviousness of the roles. As in the theatre, each physical type expresses to excess the part which has been assigned to the contestant. Thauvin, a fifty-year-old with an obese and sagging body, whose type of asexual hideousness always inspires feminine nicknames, displays in his flesh the characters of baseness, for his part is to represent what, in the classical concept of the *salaud*,[3] the "bastard" (the key-concept of any wrestling match), appears as organically repugnant. The nausea voluntarily provoked by Thauvin shows therefore a very extended use of signs: not only is ugliness used here in order to signify baseness, but in addition ugliness is wholly gathered into a particularly repulsive quality of matter: the pallid col-

---

1   *masks and buskins* The costumes for Greek tragic actors evolved to include highly stylized masks and boots called buskins, which had raised soles to make the actors appear taller.

2   *sign* Here, any unit that communicates meaning, such as a word, gesture, or image.

3   *salaud* French slang: bastard, someone despicably immoral and hypocritical.

lapse of dead flesh (the public calls Thauvin *la barbaque*, "stinking meat"), so that the passionate condemnation of the crowd no longer stems from its judgment, but instead from the very depth of its humours. It will thereafter let itself be frenetically embroiled in an idea of Thauvin which will conform entirely with this physical origin: his actions will perfectly correspond to the essential viscosity of his personage.

It is therefore in the body of the wrestler that we find the first key to the contest. I know from the start that all of Thauvin's actions, his treacheries, cruelties and acts of cowardice, will not fail to measure up to the first image of ignobility he gave me; I can trust him to carry out intelligently and to the last detail all the gestures of a kind of amorphous baseness, and thus fill to the brim the image of the most repugnant bastard there is: the bastard-octopus.... Thauvin will never be anything but an ignoble traitor, Reinières (a tall blond fellow with a limp body and unkempt hair) the moving image of passivity, Mazaud (short and arrogant like a cock) that of grotesque conceit, and Orsano (an effeminate teddy-boy first seen in a blue-and-pink dressing-gown) that, doubly humorous, of a vindictive *salope*,[1] or bitch....

The physique of the wrestlers therefore constitutes a basic sign, which like a seed contains the whole fight. But this seed proliferates, for it is at every turn during the fight, in each new situation, that the body of the wrestler casts to the public the magical entertainment of a temperament which finds its natural expression in a gesture. The different strata of meaning throw light on each other, and form the most intelligible of spectacles.... [A]bove the fundamental meaning of his body, the wrestler arranges comments which are episodic but always opportune, and constantly help the reading of the fight by means of gestures, attitudes and mimicry which make the intention utterly obvious. Sometimes the wrestler triumphs with a repulsive sneer while kneeling on the good sportsman; sometimes he gives the crowd a conceited smile which forebodes an early revenge; sometimes, pinned to the ground, he hits the floor ostentatiously to make evident to all the intolerable nature of his situation; and sometimes he erects a complicated set of signs meant to make the public understand that he legitimately personifies the ever-entertaining image of the grumbler, endlessly confabulating about his displeasure.

We are therefore dealing with a real Human Comedy, where the most socially-inspired nuances of passion (conceit, rightfulness, refined cruelty, a sense of "paying one's debts") always felicitously find the clearest sign which can receive them, express them and triumphantly carry them to the confines of the hall. It is obvious that at such a pitch, it no longer matters whether the passion is genuine or not. What the public wants is the image of passion, not pas-

---

1   *salope* French slang: bitch, slut; an insult typically directed at a woman.

sion itself. There is no more a problem of truth in wrestling than in the theatre. In both, what is expected is the intelligible representation of moral situations which are usually private. This emptying out of interiority to the benefit of its exterior signs, this exhaustion of the content by the form, is the very principle of triumphant classical art. Wrestling is an immediate pantomime, infinitely more efficient than the dramatic pantomime, for the wrestler's gesture needs no anecdote, no decor, in short no transference in order to appear true.

Each moment in wrestling is therefore like an algebra which instantaneously unveils the relationship between a cause and its represented effect. Wrestling fans certainly experience a kind of intellectual pleasure in *seeing* the moral mechanism function so perfectly. Some wrestlers, who are great comedians, entertain as much as a Molière character, because they succeed in imposing an immediate reading of their inner nature: Armand Mazaud, a wrestler of an arrogant and ridiculous character (as one says that Harpagon[1] is a character), always delights the audience by the mathematical rigour of his transcriptions, carrying the form of his gestures to the furthest reaches of their meaning, and giving to his manner of fighting a kind of vehemence and precision found in a great scholastic disputation,[2] in which what is at stake is at once the triumph of pride and the formal concern with truth.

What is thus displayed for the public is the great spectacle of Suffering, Defeat, and Justice. Wrestling presents man's suffering with all the amplification of tragic masks. The wrestler who suffers in a hold which is reputedly cruel (an arm-lock, a twisted leg) offers an excessive portrayal of Suffering; like a primitive Pietà,[3] he exhibits for all to see his face, exaggeratedly contorted by an intolerable affliction. It is obvious, of course, that in wrestling reserve would be out of place, since it is opposed to the voluntary ostentation of the spectacle, to this Exhibition of Suffering which is the very aim of the fight. This is why all the actions which produce suffering are particularly spectacular, like the gesture of a conjuror who holds out his cards clearly to the public. Suffering which appeared without intelligible cause would not be understood; a concealed action that was actually cruel would transgress the underwritten rules of wrestling and would have no more sociological efficacy than a mad or parasitic gesture. On the contrary suffering appears as inflicted with emphasis and conviction, for everyone must not only see that the man suffers, but also and above all understand why he suffers. What wrestlers call a hold, that is, any figure which allows one to immobilize the adversary indefinitely and to have him at one's mercy, has precisely the function of preparing in a conven-

---

1   *Harpagon* Stingy, old protagonist of Molière's comedy *The Miser* (1668).

2   *scholastic disputation* Formal philosophical argument of the sort conducted at medieval universities.

3   *Pietà* Work of art depicting the Virgin Mary holding Christ's dead body.

tional, therefore intelligible, fashion the spectacle of suffering, of methodically establishing the conditions of suffering. The inertia of the vanquished allows the (temporary) victor to settle in his cruelty and to convey to the public this terrifying slowness of the torturer who is certain about the outcome of his actions; to grind the face of one's powerless adversary or to scrape his spine with one's fist with a deep and regular movement, or at least to produce the superficial appearance of such gestures: wrestling is the only sport which gives such an externalized image of torture. But here again, only the image is involved in the game, and the spectator does not wish for the actual suffering of the contestant; he only enjoys the perfection of an iconography. It is not true that wrestling is a sadistic spectacle: it is only an intelligible spectacle.

There is another figure, more spectacular still than a hold; it is the forearm smash, this loud slap of the forearm, this embryonic punch with which one clouts the chest of one's adversary, and which is accompanied by a dull noise and the exaggerated sagging of a vanquished body. In the forearm smash, catastrophe is brought to the point of maximum obviousness, so much so that ultimately the gesture appears as no more than a symbol; this is going too far, this is transgressing the moral rules of wrestling, where all signs must be excessively clear, but must not let the intention of clarity be seen. The public then shouts "He's laying it on!," not because it regrets the absence of real suffering, but because it condemns artifice: as in the theatre, one fails to put the part across as much by an excess of sincerity as by an excess of formalism.

We have already seen to what extent wrestlers exploit the resources of a given physical style, developed and put to use in order to unfold before the eyes of the public a total image of Defeat. The flaccidity of tall white bodies which collapse with one blow or crash into the ropes with arms flailing, the inertia of massive wrestlers rebounding pitiably off all the elastic surfaces of the ring, nothing can signify more clearly and more passionately the exemplary abasement of the vanquished. Deprived of all resilience, the wrestler's flesh is no longer anything but an unspeakable heap spread out on the floor, where it solicits relentless reviling and jubilation. There is here a paroxysm of meaning in the style of antiquity, which can only recall the heavily underlined intentions in Roman triumphs. At other times, there is another ancient posture which appears in the coupling of the wrestlers, that of the suppliant who, at the mercy of his opponent, on bended knees, his arms raised above his head, is slowly brought down by the vertical pressure of the victor. In wrestling, unlike judo, Defeat is not a conventional sign, abandoned as soon as it is understood; it is not an outcome, but quite the contrary, it is a duration, a display, it takes up the ancient myths of public Suffering and Humiliation: the cross and the pillory. It is as if the wrestler is crucified in broad daylight and in the sight of all. I have heard it said of a wrestler stretched on the ground: "He is dead, little Jesus, there, on the cross," and these ironic words revealed the hidden roots of a spectacle which enacts the exact gestures of the most ancient purifications.

But what wrestling is above all meant to portray is a purely moral concept: that of justice. The idea of "paying" is essential to wrestling, and the crowd's "Give it to him" means above all else "Make him pay." This is therefore, needless to say, an immanent justice. The baser the action of the "bastard," the more delighted the public is by the blow which he justly receives in return. If the villain—who is of course a coward—takes refuge behind the ropes, claiming unfairly to have a right to do so by a brazen mimicry, he is inexorably pursued there and caught, and the crowd is jubilant at seeing the rules broken for the sake of a deserved punishment. Wrestlers know very well how to play up to the capacity for indignation of the public by presenting the very limit of the concept of Justice, this outermost zone of confrontation where it is enough to infringe the rules a little more to open the gates of a world without restraints. For a wrestling-fan, nothing is finer than the revengeful fury of a betrayed fighter who throws himself vehemently not on a successful opponent but on the smarting image of foul play. Naturally, it is the pattern of Justice which matters here, much more than its content: wrestling is above all a quantitative sequence of compensations (an eye for an eye, a tooth for a tooth). This explains why sudden changes of circumstances have in the eyes of wrestling habitués a sort of moral beauty: they enjoy them as they would enjoy an inspired episode in a novel, and the greater the contrast between the success of a move and the reversal of fortune, the nearer the good luck of a contestant to his downfall, the more satisfying the dramatic mime is felt to be. Justice is therefore the embodiment of a possible transgression; it is from the fact that there is a Law that the spectacle of the passions which infringe it derives its value.

It is therefore easy to understand why out of five wrestling-matches, only about one is fair. One must realize, let it be repeated, that "fairness" here is a role or a genre, as in the theatre: the rules do not at all constitute a real constraint; they are the conventional appearance of fairness. So that in actual fact a fair fight is nothing but an exaggeratedly polite one: the contestants confront each other with zeal, not rage; they can remain in control of their passions, they do not punish their beaten opponent relentlessly, they stop fighting as soon as they are ordered to do so, and congratulate each other at the end of a particularly arduous episode, during which, however, they have not ceased to be fair. One must of course understand here that all these polite actions are brought to the notice of the public by the most conventional gestures of fairness: shaking hands, raising the arms, ostensibly avoiding a fruitless hold which would detract from the perfection of the contest.

Conversely, foul play exists only in its excessive signs: administering a big kick to one's beaten opponent, taking refuge behind the ropes while ostensibly invoking a purely formal right, refusing to shake hands with one's opponent before or after the fight, taking advantage of the end of the round to rush treacherously at the adversary from behind, fouling him while the referee is not looking (a move which obviously only has any value or function because in fact half the audience can see it and get indignant about it). Since Evil is the natural climate of wrestling, a fair fight has chiefly the value of being an exception. It surprises the aficionado, who greets it when he sees it as an anachronism and a rather sentimental throwback to the sporting tradition ("Aren't they playing fair, those two"); he feels suddenly moved at the sight of the general kindness of the world, but would probably die of boredom and indifference if wrestlers did not quickly return to the orgy of evil which alone makes good wrestling.

Extrapolated, fair wrestling could lead only to boxing or judo, whereas true wrestling derives its originality from all the excesses which make it a spectacle and not a sport. The ending of a boxing-match or a judo-contest is abrupt, like the full-stop which closes a demonstration. The rhythm of wrestling is quite different, for its natural meaning is that of rhetorical amplification: the emotional magniloquence,[1] the repeated paroxysms, the exasperation of the retorts can only find their natural outcome in the most baroque confusion. Some fights, among the most successful kind, are crowned by a final charivari,[2] a sort of unrestrained fantasia where the rules, the laws of the genre, the referee's censuring and the limits of the ring are abolished, swept away by a triumphant disorder which overflows into the hall and carries off pell-mell wrestlers, seconds, referee and spectators....

What then is a "bastard" for this audience composed in part, we are told, of people who are themselves outside the rules of society? Essentially someone unstable, who accepts the rules only when they are useful to him and transgresses the formal continuity of attitudes. He is unpredictable, therefore asocial. He takes refuge behind the law when he considers that it is in his favour, and breaks it when he finds it useful to do so. Sometimes he rejects the formal boundaries of the ring and goes on hitting an adversary legally protected by the ropes, sometimes he reestablishes these boundaries and claims the protection of what he did not respect a few minutes earlier. This inconsistency, far more than treachery or cruelty, sends the audience beside itself with rage: offended not in its morality but in its logic, it considers the contradiction of arguments as the basest of crimes. The forbidden move becomes dirty only when it de-

---

1   *magniloquence* Excessive pomposity, usually in reference to speech or writing.
2   *charivari* Raucous procession of people making discordant noise by shouting, banging objects, blowing whistles, etc.

stroys a quantitative equilibrium and disturbs the rigorous reckoning of compensations; what is condemned by the audience is not at all the transgression of insipid official rules, it is the lack of revenge, the absence of a punishment. So that there is nothing more exciting for a crowd than the grandiloquent kick given to a vanquished "bastard"; the joy of punishing is at its climax when it is supported by a mathematical justification; contempt is then unrestrained. One is no longer dealing with a *salaud* but with a *salope*—the verbal gesture of the ultimate degradation.

Such a precise finality demands that wrestling should be exactly what the public expects of it. Wrestlers, who are very experienced, know perfectly how to direct the spontaneous episodes of the fight so as to make them conform to the image which the public has of the great legendary themes of its mythology. A wrestler can irritate or disgust, he never disappoints, for he always accomplishes completely, by a progressive solidification of signs, what the public expects of him. In wrestling, nothing exists except in the absolute, there is no symbol, no allusion, everything is presented exhaustively. Leaving nothing in the shade, each action discards all parasitic meanings and ceremonially offers to the public a pure and full signification, rounded like Nature. This grandiloquence is nothing but the popular and age-old image of the perfect intelligibility of reality. What is portrayed by wrestling is therefore an ideal understanding of things; it is the euphoria of men raised for a while above the constitutive ambiguity of everyday situations and placed before the panoramic view of a univocal Nature, in which signs at last correspond to causes, without obstacle, without evasion, without contradiction.

When the hero or the villain of the drama, the man who was seen a few minutes earlier possessed by moral rage, magnified into a sort of metaphysical sign, leaves the wrestling hall, impassive, anonymous, carrying a small suitcase and arm-in-arm with his wife, no one can doubt that wrestling holds that power of transmutation which is common to the Spectacle and to Religious Worship. In the ring, and even in the depths of their voluntary ignominy, wrestlers remain gods because they are, for a few moments, the key which opens Nature, the pure gesture which separates Good from Evil, and unveils the form of a Justice which is at last intelligible.

—1972

Philip Gourevitch
b. 1961

Philip Gourevitch is an American non-fiction writer and journalist. A staff writer for *The New Yorker* since 1997, he has travelled the world and reported on subjects such as genocide and war crimes, torture, terrorism, new political movements, and daily life in zones of conflict.

Born in Philadelphia and raised in central Connecticut, Gourevitch received a BA from Cornell University and an MFA from the Writing Program at Columbia. In addition to *The New Yorker*, he has published in *Granta*, *Harper's*, *The New York Times Magazine*, and *The New York Review of Books*. From 2005 to 2010, he served as editor of *The Paris Review*.

Gourevitch's third book, *Standard Operating Procedure* (2008), provides a "thorough, terrifying account" of a turning point in the Iraq War: the Abu Ghraib photographs of prisoner abuse. His second book, *Cold Case* (2001), reopens an investigation into a New York City double homicide that went unsolved for 30 years. But it was Gourevitch's first book that established him as one of the leading voices of his generation. *We Wish to Inform You That Tomorrow We Will Be Killed with Our Families* (1998) won many awards and has received wide recognition for shedding new light on the Rwandan genocide of 1994.

We Wish to Inform You contains visceral retellings of stories from individual Rwandan men and women. On six trips over nine months, Gourevitch gathered these stories on the ground. "Filled with empathy instead of cautious neutrality, and written in powerful muckraking prose, Gourevitch's book gives free rein to the anger—against both perpetrators and the international community—that others hold in check," wrote José E. Alvarez in *The American Journal of International Law*.

from *We Wish to Inform You That Tomorrow We Will Be Killed with Our Families*

In the Province of Kibungo, in eastern Rwanda, in the swamp- and pastureland near the Tanzanian border, there's a rocky hill called Nyarubuye with a church where many Tutsis[1] were slaughtered in mid-April of 1994. A year after the

---

1   *Tutsis* African ethnic group living primarily within Rwanda and neighbouring Burundi. In pre-colonial Rwanda, the Tutsis dominated the Hutu, an ethnic group constituting the majority of Rwanda's population. When the nation was controlled by European colonial powers—first Germany beginning in 1894, then Belgium after World War I—these governments reinforced the privilege of the Tutsis, exacerbating pre-existing ethnic tensions. The Hutu seized power from the Tutsis just before Rwanda achieved independence in

killing I went to Nyarubuye with two Canadian military officers. We flew in a United Nations helicopter, travelling low over the hills in the morning mists, with the banana trees like green starbursts dense over the slopes. The uncut grass blew back as we dropped into the centre of the parish schoolyard. A lone soldier materialized with his Kalashnikov, and shook our hands with stiff, shy formality. The Canadians presented the paperwork for our visit, and I stepped up into the open doorway of a classroom.

At least fifty mostly decomposed cadavers covered the floor, wadded in clothing, their belongings strewn about and smashed. Macheted[1] skulls had rolled here and there.

The dead looked like pictures of the dead. They did not smell. They did not buzz with flies. They had been killed thirteen months earlier, and they hadn't been moved. Skin stuck here and there over the bones, many of which lay scattered away from the bodies, dismembered by the killers, or by scavengers—birds, dogs, bugs. The more complete figures looked a lot like people, which they were once. A woman in a cloth wrap printed with flowers lay near the door. Her fleshless hip bones were high and her legs slightly spread, and a child's skeleton extended between them. Her torso was hollowed out. Her ribs and spinal column poked through the rotting cloth. Her head was tipped back and her mouth was open: a strange image—half agony, half repose.

I had never been among the dead before. What to do? Look? Yes. I wanted to see them, I suppose; I had come to see them—the dead had been left unburied at Nyarubuye for memorial purposes—and there they were, so intimately exposed. I didn't need to see them. I already knew, and believed, what had happened in Rwanda. Yet looking at the buildings and the bodies, and hearing the silence of the place, with the grand Italianate basilica standing there deserted, and beds of exquisite, decadent, death-fertilized flowers blooming over the corpses, it was still strangely unimaginable. I mean one still had to imagine it.

Those dead Rwandans will be with me forever, I expect. That was why I had felt compelled to come to Nyarubuye: to be stuck with them—not with their experience, but with the experience of looking at them. They had been killed there, and they were dead there. What else could you really see at first? The Bible bloated with rain lying on top of one corpse or, littered about, the little woven wreaths of thatch which Rwandan women wear as crowns to balance the enormous loads they carry on their heads, and the water gourds, and the Converse tennis sneaker stuck somehow in a pelvis.

1962, and ongoing conflict culminated in the Rwandan genocide, which lasted from April to mid-July in 1994. During the genocide, Hutu militias killed between 500,000 and 1 million Tutsis.

1   *macheted* The machete—a large cleaver, intended for cutting jungle brush—was commonly used as a weapon during the genocide.

The soldier with the Kalashnikov—Sergeant Francis of the Rwandese Patriotic Army,[1] a Tutsi whose parents had fled to Uganda with him when he was a boy, after similar but less extensive massacres in the early 1960s, and who had fought his way home in 1994 and found it like this—said that the dead in this room were mostly women who had been raped before being murdered. Sergeant Francis had high, rolling girlish hips, and he walked and stood with his butt stuck out behind him, an oddly purposeful posture, tipped forward, driven. He was, at once, candid and briskly official. His English had the punctilious clip of military drill, and after he told me what I was looking at I looked instead at my feet. The rusty head of a hatchet lay beside them in the dirt.

A few weeks earlier, in Bukavu, Zaire, in the giant market of a refugee camp that was home to many Rwandan Hutu militiamen, I had watched a man butchering a cow with a machete. He was quite expert at his work, taking big precise strokes that made a sharp hacking noise. The rallying cry to the killers during the genocide was "Do your work!" And I saw that it *was* work, this butchery; hard work. It took many hacks—two, three, four, five hard hacks— to chop through the cow's leg. How many hacks to dismember a person?

Considering the enormity of the task, it is tempting to play with theories of collective madness, mob mania, a fever of hatred erupted into a mass crime of passion, and to imagine the blind orgy of the mob, with each member killing one or two people. But at Nyarubuye, and at thousands of other sites in this tiny country, on the same days of a few months in 1994, hundreds of thousands of Hutus had worked as killers in regular shifts. There was always the next victim, and the next. What sustained them, beyond the frenzy of the first attack, through the plain physical exhaustion and mess of it?

The pygmy in Gikongoro said that humanity is part of nature and that we must go against nature to get along and have peace. But mass violence, too, must be organized; it does not occur aimlessly. Even mobs and riots have a design, and great and sustained destruction requires great ambition. It must be conceived as the means toward achieving a new order, and although the idea behind that new order may be criminal and objectively very stupid, it must also be compellingly simple and at the same time absolute. The ideology of genocide is all of those things, and in Rwanda it went by the bald name of Hutu Power.[2] For those who set about systematically exterminating an entire

---

1   *Rwandese Patriotic Army* Armed forces of the Rwandese Patriotic Front (RPF), a leftist political party largely composed of Tutsis, which took power in Rwanda in the aftermath of the genocide. The genocide itself was triggered when Hutu extremists accused the RPF of assassinating Rwandan president Juvénal Habyarimana and Burundian president Cyprien Ntaryamira on 6 April 1994.

2   *Hutu Power* Ideology that asserted the superiority of Hutu people and the inferiority of the Tutsis.

people—even a fairly small and unresisting subpopulation of perhaps a million and a quarter men, women, and children, like the Tutsis in Rwanda—blood lust surely helps. But the engineers and perpetrators of a slaughter like the one just inside the door where I stood need not enjoy killing, and they may even find it unpleasant. What is required above all is that they want their victims dead. They have to want it so badly that they consider it a necessity.

So I still had much to imagine as I entered the classroom and stepped carefully between the remains. These dead and their killers had been neighbours, schoolmates, colleagues, sometimes friends, even in-laws. The dead had seen their killers training as militias in the weeks before the end, and it was well known that they were training to kill Tutsis; it was announced on the radio, it was in the newspapers, people spoke of it openly. The week before the massacre at Nyarubuye, the killing began in Rwanda's capital, Kigali. Hutus who opposed the Hutu Power ideology were publicly denounced as "accomplices" of the Tutsis and were among the first to be killed as the extermination got under way. In Nyarubuye, when Tutsis asked the Hutu Power mayor how they might be spared, he suggested that they seek sanctuary at the church. They did, and a few days later the mayor came to kill them. He came at the head of a pack of soldiers, policemen, militiamen, and villagers; he gave out arms and orders to complete the job well. No more was required of the mayor, but he was also said to have killed a few Tutsis himself.

The killers killed all day at Nyarubuye. At night they cut the Achilles tendons of survivors and went off to feast behind the church, roasting cattle looted from their victims in big fires, and drinking beer. (Bottled beer, banana beer—Rwandans may not drink more beer than other Africans, but they drink prodigious quantities of it around the clock.) And, in the morning, still drunk after whatever sleep they could find beneath the cries of their prey, the killers at Nyarubuye went back and killed again. Day after day, minute to minute, Tutsi by Tutsi: all across Rwanda, they worked like that. "It was a process," Sergeant Francis said. I can see that it happened, I can be told how, and after nearly three years of looking around Rwanda and listening to Rwandans, I can tell you how, and I will. But the horror of it—the idiocy, the waste, the sheer wrongness—remains uncircumscribable.

Like Leontius,[1] the young Athenian in Plato, I presume that you are reading this because you desire a closer look, and that you, too, are properly disturbed by your curiosity. Perhaps, in examining this extremity with me, you hope for some understanding, some insight, some flicker of self-knowledge—a

---

1   *Leontius* Character referred to in Plato's *Republic* (c. 380 BCE) who was reputedly unable to resist staring at a heap of dead bodies. Plato's Socrates tells the story of Leontius in order to illustrate the compulsiveness and irrationality of the appetitive—i.e., desiring—aspect of the human soul.

moral, or a lesson, or a clue about how to behave in this world: some such information. I don't discount the possibility, but when it comes to genocide, you already know right from wrong. The best reason I have come up with for looking closely into Rwanda's stories is that ignoring them makes me even more uncomfortable about existence and my place in it. The horror, as horror, interests me only insofar as a precise memory of the offence is necessary to understand its legacy.

The dead at Nyarubuye were, I'm afraid, beautiful. There was no getting around it. The skeleton is a beautiful thing. The randomness of the fallen forms, the strange tranquility of their rude exposure, the skull here, the arm bent in some uninterpretable gesture there—these things were beautiful, and their beauty only added to the affront of the place. I couldn't settle on any meaningful response: revulsion, alarm, sorrow, grief, shame, incomprehension, sure, but nothing truly meaningful. I just looked, and I took photographs, because I wondered whether I could really see what I was seeing while I saw it, and I wanted also an excuse to look a bit more closely.

We went on through the first room and out the far side. There was another room and another and another and another. They were all full of bodies, and more bodies were scattered in the grass and there were stray skulls in the grass, which was thick and wonderfully green. Standing outside, I heard a crunch. The old Canadian colonel stumbled in front of me, and I saw, though he did not notice, that his foot had rolled on a skull and broken it. For the first time at Nyarubuye my feelings focused, and what I felt was a small but keen anger at this man. Then I heard another crunch, and felt a vibration underfoot. I had stepped on one, too.

Rwanda is spectacular to behold. Throughout its centre, a winding succession of steep, tightly terraced slopes radiates out from small roadside settlements and solitary compounds. Gashes of red clay and black loam mark fresh hoe work; eucalyptus trees flash silver against brilliant green tea plantations; banana trees are everywhere. On the theme of hills, Rwanda produces countless variations: jagged rain forests, round-shouldered buttes, undulating moors, broad swells of savanna, volcanic peaks sharp as filed teeth. During the rainy season, the clouds are huge and low and fast, mists cling in highland hollows, lightning flickers through the nights, and by day the land is lustrous. After the rains, the skies lift, the terrain takes on a ragged look beneath the flat unvarying haze of the dry season, and in the savannas of the Akagera Park wildlife blackens the hills.

One day, when I was returning to Kigali from the south, the car mounted a rise between two winding valleys, the windshield filled with purple-bellied clouds, and I asked Joseph, the man who was giving me a ride, whether Rwandans realize what a beautiful country they have. "Beautiful?" he said. "You think so? After the things that happened here? The people aren't good. If the people were good, the country might be OK." Joseph told me that his brother and sister had been killed, and he made a soft hissing click with his tongue against his teeth. "The country is empty," he said. "Empty!"

It was not just the dead who were missing. The genocide had been brought to a halt by the Rwandese Patriotic Front, a rebel army led by Tutsi refugees from past persecutions, and as the RPF advanced through the country in the summer of 1994, some two million Hutus had fled into exile at the behest of the same leaders who had urged them to kill. Yet except in some rural areas in the south, where the desertion of Hutus had left nothing but bush to reclaim the fields around crumbling adobe houses, I, as a newcomer, could not see the emptiness that blinded Joseph to Rwanda's beauty. Yes, there were grenade-flattened buildings, burnt homesteads, shot-up facades, and mortar-pitted roads. But these were the ravages of war, not of genocide, and by the summer of 1995, most of the dead had been buried. Fifteen months earlier, Rwanda had been the most densely populated country in Africa. Now the work of the killers looked just as they had intended: invisible.

From time to time, mass graves were discovered and excavated, and the remains would be transferred to new, properly consecrated mass graves. Yet even the occasionally exposed bones, the conspicuous number of amputees and people with deforming scars, and the superabundance of packed orphanages could not be taken as evidence that what had happened to Rwanda was an attempt to eliminate a people. There were only people's stories.

"Every survivor wonders why he is alive," Abbé Modeste, a priest at the cathedral in Butare, Rwanda's second-largest city, told me. Abbé Modeste had hidden for weeks in his sacristy,[1] eating communion wafers, before moving under the desk in his study, and finally into the rafters at the home of some neighbouring nuns. The obvious explanation of his survival was that the RPF had come to the rescue. But the RPF didn't reach Butare till early July, and roughly seventy-five percent of the Tutsis in Rwanda had been killed by early May. In this regard, at least, the genocide had been entirely successful: to those who were targeted, it was not death but life that seemed an accident of fate.

"I had eighteen people killed at my house," said Etienne Niyonzima, a former businessman who had become a deputy in the National Assembly. "Everything was totally destroyed—a place of fifty-five metres by fifty metres. In my neighbourhood they killed six hundred and forty-seven people. They tortured them, too. You had to see how they killed them. They had the number

---

1   *sacristy* Room in a Christian church where priests and attendants prepare for mass or other religious services.

of everyone's house, and they went through with red paint and marked the homes of all the Tutsis and of the Hutu moderates. My wife was at a friend's, shot with two bullets. She is still alive, only"—he fell quiet for a moment— "she has no arms. The others with her were killed. The militia left her for dead. Her whole family of sixty-five in Gitarama were killed." Niyonzima was in hiding at the time. Only after he had been separated from his wife for three months did he learn that she and four of their children had survived. "Well," he said, "one son was cut in the head with a machete. I don't know where he went." His voice weakened, and caught. "He disappeared." Niyonzima clicked his tongue, and said, "But the others are still alive. Quite honestly, I don't understand at all how I was saved."

Laurent Nkongoli attributed his survival to "Providence,[1] and also good neighbours, an old woman who said, 'Run away, we don't want to see your corpse.'" Nkongoli, a lawyer, who had become the vice president of the National Assembly after the genocide, was a robust man, with a taste for double-breasted suit jackets and lively ties, and he moved, as he spoke, with a brisk determination. But before taking his neighbour's advice, and fleeing Kigali in late April of 1994, he said, "I had accepted death. At a certain moment this happens. One hopes not to die cruelly, but one expects to die anyway. Not death by machete, one hopes, but with a bullet. If you were willing to pay for it, you could often ask for a bullet. Death was more or less normal, a resignation. You lose the will to fight. There were four thousand Tutsis killed here at Kacyiru"—a neighbourhood of Kigali. "The soldiers brought them here, and told them to sit down because they were going to throw grenades. And they sat.

"Rwandan culture is a culture of fear," Nkongoli went on. "I remember what people said." He adopted a pipey voice, and his face took on a look of disgust: "'Just let us pray, then kill us,' or 'I don't want to die in the street, I want to die at home.'" He resumed his normal voice. "When you're that resigned and oppressed you're already dead. It shows the genocide was prepared for too long. I detest this fear. These victims of genocide had been psychologically prepared to expect death just for being Tutsi. They were being killed for so long that they were already dead."

I reminded Nkongoli that, for all his hatred of fear, he had himself accepted death before his neighbour urged him to run away. "Yes," he said. "I got tired in the genocide. You struggle so long, then you get tired."

Every Rwandan I spoke with seemed to have a favourite, unanswerable question. For Nkongoli, it was how so many Tutsis had allowed themselves to be killed. For François Xavier Nkurunziza, a Kigali lawyer, whose father was Hutu and whose mother and wife were Tutsi, the question was how so many

---

1   *Providence* God's will, divine intervention.

Hutus had allowed themselves to kill. Nkurunziza had escaped death only by chance as he moved around the country from one hiding place to another, and he had lost many family members. "Conformity is very deep, very developed here," he told me. "In Rwandan history, everyone obeys authority. People revere power, and there isn't enough education. You take a poor, ignorant population, and give them arms, and say, 'It's yours. Kill.' They'll obey. The peasants, who were paid or forced to kill, were looking up to people of higher socio-economic standing to see how to behave. So the people of influence, or the big financiers, are often the big men in the genocide. They may think they didn't kill because they didn't take life with their own hands, but the people were looking to them for their orders. And, in Rwanda, an order can be given very quietly."

As I travelled around the country, collecting accounts of the killing, it almost seemed as if, with the machete, the *masu*—a club studded with nails—a few well-placed grenades, and a few bursts of automatic-rifle fire, the quiet orders of Hutu Power had made the neutron bomb[1] obsolete.

"Everyone was called to hunt the enemy," said Theodore Nyilinkwaya, a survivor of the massacres in his home village of Kimbogo, in the southwestern province of Cyangugu. "But let's say someone is reluctant. Say that guy comes with a stick. They tell him, 'No, get a *masu*.' So, OK, he does, and he runs along with the rest, but he doesn't kill. They say, 'Hey, he might denounce us later. He must kill. Everyone must help to kill at least one person.' So this person who is not a killer is made to do it. And the next day it's become a game for him. You don't need to keep pushing him."

At Nyarubuye, even the little terracotta votive statues[2] in the sacristy had been methodically decapitated. "They were associated with Tutsis," Sergeant Francis explained.

—1999

---

1   *neutron bomb* Thermonuclear weapon that releases a small amount of explosive energy, but an enormous amount of radiation. A neutron bomb does very little damage to infrastructure, but incredible damage to a human population.

2   *votive statues* Statues intended to be used as religious offerings.

Drew Hayden Taylor
b. 1962

Drew Hayden Taylor is a Canadian author who works in a variety of literary genres, though he is best known as a playwright. His award winning plays include *Toronto at Dreamer's Rock* (1990), *The Bootlegger Blues* (1991), and *Only Drunks and Children Tell the Truth* (1998). An Ojibway from the Curve Lake First Nation in Ontario, he is recognized as an important Aboriginal voice in the Canadian literary world. In addition to writing plays, he has served as the artistic director of Toronto's Native Earth Performing Arts theatre company, taught at the Centre for Indigenous Theatre, and served as Writer in Residence at the University of Michigan, the University of Western Ontario, the University of Luneburg (Germany), and several Canadian theatre companies.

Taylor has also written short stories and television and film scripts, and has contributed to numerous documentaries. In 2007, he published his first novel, the youth-oriented vampire tale *The Night Wanderer: A Native Gothic Novel* (2007). This was soon followed by his first novel for adults, *Motorcycles & Sweetgrass* (2010), which was nominated for the Governor General's Award for Fiction and earned him recognition as one of Random House Canada's 2010 New Faces of Fiction. He regularly contributes columns and articles to newspapers and magazines.

Central to this diverse body of work is Taylor's sensitivity to the demands of effective storytelling and his desire to convey an Aboriginal perspective in an honest and engaging way. In his words, "My whole philosophy as a writer is to create interesting characters, with an interesting story, and to take the audience on an interesting journey." Regarding the goals of his work, he has said, "I hope that I have provided a window of understanding between Native and non-Native cultures by demystifying Native life."

Pretty Like a White Boy

In this big, huge world, with all its billions and billions of people, it's safe to say that everybody will eventually come across personalities and individuals who will touch them in some peculiar yet poignant way. Characters that in some way represent and help define who you are. I'm no different—mine is Kermit the Frog. Not just because Natives have a long tradition of savouring frogs' legs, but because of this particular frog's music. You all may remember Kermit is quite famous for his rendition of *It's Not Easy Being Green*. I can relate. If I could sing, my song would be *It's Not Easy Having Blue Eyes in a Brown-Eyed Village*.

Yes, I'm afraid it's true. The author happens to be a card-carrying Indian. Once you get past the aforementioned eyes, the fair skin, light brown hair and noticeable lack of cheek bones, there lies the heart and spirit of an Ojibway storyteller. "Honest Injun" or as the more politically correct term may be, "Honest Aboriginal."

You see, I'm the product of a White father I never knew and an Ojibway woman who evidently couldn't run fast enough. As a kid I knew I looked a bit different but, then again, all kids are paranoid when it comes to their peers. I had a fairly happy childhood, frolicking through the bulrushes. But there were certain things that even then made me notice my unusual appearance. Whenever we played cowboys and Indians, guess who had to be the bad guy (the cowboy)?

It wasn't until I left the reserve for the big bad city, that I became more aware of the role people expected me to play, and the fact that physically, I didn't fit in. Everybody seemed to have this preconceived idea of how every Indian looked and acted. One guy, on my first day of college, asked me what kind of horse I preferred. I didn't have the heart to tell him "hobby."

I've often tried to be philosophical about the whole thing. I have both White and Red blood in me. I guess that makes me pink. I am a "Pink Man." Try to imagine this: I'm walking around on any typical reserve in Canada, my head held high, proudly announcing to everyone, "I am a Pink Man." It's a good thing I ran track in school.

My pinkness is constantly being pointed out to me over and over and over again. "You don't look Indian!" "You're not Indian, are you?" "Really?!?!" I got questions like that from both White and Native people. For a while I debated having my Status card tattooed on my forehead.

And like most insecure people, and especially a blue-eyed Native writer, I went through a particularly severe identity crisis at one point. In fact, I admit it, one depressing spring evening I dyed my hair black. Pitch black.

The reason for such a dramatic act, you ask? Show business. You see, for the last eight years or so, I've worked in various capacities in the performing arts, and as a result I often get calls to be an extra or even try out for an important role in some Native-oriented movie. This anonymous voice would phone, having been given my number, and ask if I would be interested in trying out for a movie. Being a naturally ambitious, curious and greedy young man, I would always readily agree, stardom flashing in my eyes and hunger pains calling from my wallet.

A few days later I would show up for the audition, and that was always an experience. What kind of experience you ask? Picture this: the movie calls for the casting of seventeenth century Mohawk warriors living in a traditional longhouse. The casting director calls the name Drew Hayden Taylor, and I enter. The casting director, the producer and the film's director look up and see my face, blue eyes shining in anticipation. I once was described as a slightly chubby beach boy. But even beach boys have tans. Anyway, there would be a quick flush of confusion, a recheck of the papers and a hesitant "Mr. Taylor?" Then they would ask if I was at the right audition. It was always the same. By the way, I never got any of the parts I tried for except for a few anonymous crowd shots. Politics tell me it's because of the way I look, reality tells me it's probably because I can't act. I'm not sure which is better.

It's not just film people either. Recently I've become quite involved in theatre—Native theatre to be exact. And one cold October day I was happily attending the Toronto leg of a province-wide tour of my first play, *Toronto at Dreamer's Rock*. The place was sold out, the audience very receptive, and the performance was wonderful. Ironically one of the actors was also half-White. The director later told me he had been talking with that actor's father, an older non-Native chap. Evidently he had asked a few questions about me, and how I did my research. This made the director curious and he asked about the man's interest. He replied, "He's got an amazing grasp of the Native situation for a White person."

Not all these incidents are work-related either. One time a friend and I were coming out of a rather up-scale bar (we were out yuppie-watching) and managed to catch a cab. We thanked the cab driver for being so comfortably close on such a cold night. He shrugged and nonchalantly talked about knowing what bars to drive around. "If you're not careful, all you'll get is drunk Indians." I hiccuped.

Another time, the cab driver droned on and on about the government. He started out by criticizing Mulroney himself, and then eventually, his handling of the Oka crisis.[1] This perked up my ears, until he said, "If it were me, I'd have tear-gassed the place by the second day. No more problems." He got a dime tip. A few incidents like this and I'm convinced I'd make a great undercover agent for Native political organizations.

But then again, even Native people have been known to look at me with a fair amount of suspicion. Many years ago when I was a young man, I was working on a documentary on Native culture up in the wilds of northern Ontario. We were at an isolated cabin filming a trapper woman and her kids. This one particular nine-year-old girl seemed to take a shine to me. She followed me around for two days, both annoying me and endearing herself to me. But she absolutely refused to believe that I was Indian. The whole film crew

---

1   *Mulroney* Brian Mulroney, prime minister of Canada from 1984 to 1993; *Oka crisis* Mohawk protest over disputed land that developed into a violent conflict with government military and police forces. Protesters occupied the disputed land—which the town of Oka, Quebec, wanted to use for a golf course—from July to September in 1990.

tried to tell her but to no avail. She was certain I was White. Then one day as I was loading up the car with film equipment, she asked me if I wanted some tea. Being in a hurry, I declined the tea. She immediately smiled with victory, crying out, "See, you're not Indian. All Indians drink tea!"

Frustrated and a little hurt, I whipped out my Status card and showed it to her. Now there I was, standing in a northern Ontario winter, showing my Status card to a nine-year-old, non-status, Indian girl who had no idea what it was. Looking back, this may not have been one of my brighter moves.

But I must admit, it was a Native woman that boiled everything down to one simple sentence. You may know that woman—Marianne Jones from *The Beachcombers*[1] television series. We were working on a film together out west and we got to gossiping. Eventually we got around to talking about our respective villages. Her village is on the Queen Charlotte Islands, or Haida Gwaii as the Haida call them, and mine is in central Ontario.

Eventually, childhood on the reserve was being discussed and I made a comment about the way I look. She studied me for a moment, smiled and said, "Do you know what the old women in my village would call you?" Hesitant but curious, I shook my head. "They'd say you were pretty like a White boy." To this day I'm still not sure if I like that.

Now some may argue that I am simply a Métis with a Status card. I disagree—I failed French in grade eleven. And the Métis, as everyone knows, have their own separate and honourable culture, particularly in western Canada. And, of course, I am well aware that I am not the only person with my physical characteristics.

I remember once looking at a video tape of a drum group, shot on a reserve up near Manitoulin Island. I noticed one of the drummers seemed quite fair-haired, almost blond. I mentioned this to my girlfriend of the time and she shrugged, saying, "Well, that's to be expected. The highway runs right through that reserve."

Perhaps I'm being too critical. There's a lot to be said for both cultures. For example, on the one hand, you have the Native respect for Elders. They understand the concept of wisdom and insight coming with age.

On the White hand, there's Italian food. I mean I really love my mother and family but seriously, does anything really beat good Veal Scaloppine? Most of my Aboriginal friends share my fondness for this particular type of food. Wasn't there a warrior at Oka named Lasagna? I found it ironic, though curiously logical, that Columbus was Italian. A connection, I wonder?

---

1   *Marianne Jones* Haida filmmaker and actor; *The Beachcombers* Canadian television series (1972–90) set in Gibsons, British Columbia.

Also, Native people have this wonderful respect and love for the land. They believe they are part of it, a mere link in the cycle of existence. Now as many of you know, this clashes with the accepted Judeo-Christian (i.e. western) view of land management. I even believe somewhere in the first chapters of the Bible it says something about God giving man dominion over nature. Check it out, Genesis 4 (?) "Thou shalt clear cut." But I grew up understanding that everything around me is important and alive. My Native heritage gave me that.

And again, on the White hand, there are breast implants. Darn clever them White people. That's something Indians would never have invented, seriously. We're not ambitious enough. We just take what the Creator decides to give us; but no, not the White man. Just imagine it, some serious looking White doctor (and let's face it people, we know it was a man who invented them) sitting around in his laboratory muttering to himself, "Big tits, big tits, hmm, how do I make big tits?" If it was an Indian, it would be, "Big tits, big tits, White women sure got big tits," and leave it at that.

So where does that leave me on the big philosophical score board? What exactly are my choices again? Indians: respect for Elders, love of the land. White people: food and big tits. In order to live in both cultures I guess I'd have to find an Indian woman with big tits who lives with her grandmother in a cabin out in the woods and can make Fettuccini Alfredo on a wood stove.

Now let me make myself clear—I'm not writing this for sympathy, or out of anger, or even some need for self-glorification. I am just setting the facts straight. For as you read this, a new Nation is born. This is a declaration of independence. My declaration of independence.

I've spent too many years explaining who and what I am repeatedly, so, as of this moment, I officially secede from both races. I plan to start my own separate nation. Because I am half Ojibway and half Caucasian, we will be called the Occasions. And of course, since I'm founding the new nation, I will be a Special Occasion.

—1991

David Foster Wallace

1962–2008

David Foster Wallace was an American writer of novels, essays, and short stories. The publication of his novel *Infinite Jest* (1996) catapulted him to national prominence as a writer; in 2005, *Time* magazine included it in their list of the "100 Best English-language Novels Published Since 1923." Wallace's essays—notably "Consider the Lobster" (2004) and "A Supposedly Fun Thing I'll Never Do Again" (1996)—are also widely referenced and anthologized; he has come to be recognized as an important writer in multiple literary genres.

Wallace's father was a professor of philosophy, and his mother was a professor of English; given that background, it is perhaps not surprising that Wallace's approach is both cerebral and consciously literary. His writing style is inquisitive, elliptical, and sometimes playful, but there is a deep seriousness to it; questions about the nature of human experience and the functioning of society lie at the heart of much of his writing, which displays a philosopher's resistance to final and certain answers. He has said that "part of our emergency is that it's so tempting … to retreat to narrow arrogance, pre-formed positions, rigid filters, the 'moral clarity' of the immature. The alternative is dealing with massive, high-entropy amounts of info and ambiguity and conflict and flux." Reflecting this dilemma, his texts are often wildly discursive—peppered with asides, qualifications, and tangential discussions. *Infinite Jest*, for example, has hundreds of endnotes, many of which are themselves further annotated. The essay collected here, "Consider the Lobster," also employs notes extensively.

Wallace committed suicide in 2008 after a life-long battle with depression, leaving behind an unfinished manuscript for the novel *The Pale King* (2011). That the unfinished novel became a finalist for the 2012 Pulitzer Prize in fiction testifies to Wallace's important place in the literary world.

Consider the Lobster

The enormous, pungent, and extremely well-marketed Maine Lobster Festival is held every late July in the state's midcoast region, meaning the western side of Penobscot Bay, the nerve stem of Maine's lobster industry. What's called the midcoast runs from Owl's Head and Thomaston in the south to Belfast in the north. (Actually, it might extend all the way up to Bucksport, but we were never able to get farther north than Belfast on Route 1, whose summer traffic is, as you can imagine, unimaginable.) The region's two main communities are Camden, with its very old money and yachty harbour and five-star restaurants and phenomenal B&Bs, and Rockland, a serious old fishing town that hosts the festival every summer in historic Harbor Park, right along the water.[1]

Tourism and lobster are the midcoast region's two main industries, and they're both warm-weather enterprises, and the Maine Lobster Festival represents less an intersection of the industries than a deliberate collision, joyful and lucrative and loud. The assigned subject of this *Gourmet* article[2] is the 56th Annual MLF, 30 July–3 August, 2003, whose official theme this year was "Lighthouses, Laughter, and Lobster." Total paid attendance was over 100,000, due partly to a national CNN spot in June during which a senior editor of *Food & Wine* magazine hailed the MLF as one of the best food-themed galas in the world. 2003 festival highlights: concerts by Lee Ann Womack and Orleans,[3] annual Maine Sea Goddess beauty pageant, Saturday's big parade, Sunday's William G. Atwood Memorial Crate Race, annual Amateur Cooking Competition, carnival rides and midway attractions and food booths, and the MLF's Main Eating Tent, where something over 25,000 pounds of fresh-caught Maine lobster is consumed after preparation in the World's Largest Lobster Cooker near the grounds' north entrance. Also available are lobster rolls, lobster turnovers, lobster sauté, Down East lobster salad, lobster bisque, lobster ravioli, and deep-fried lobster dumplings. Lobster thermidor[4] is obtainable at a sit-down restaurant called the Black Pearl on Harbor Park's northwest wharf. A large all-pine booth sponsored by the Maine Lobster Promotion Council has free pamphlets with recipes, eating tips, and Lobster Fun Facts. The winner of Friday's Amateur Cooking Competition prepares Saffron Lobster Ramekins, the recipe for which is now available for public downloading at www.mainelobsterfestival.com. There are lobster T-shirts and lobster bobblehead dolls and inflatable lobster pool toys and clamp-on lobster hats with big scarlet claws that wobble on springs. Your assigned correspondent saw it all, accompanied by one girlfriend and both his own parents—one of which parents was actually born and raised in Maine, albeit in the extreme northern inland part, which is potato country and a world away from the touristic midcoast.[5]

For practical purposes, everyone knows what a lobster is. As usual, though, there's much more to know than most of us care about—it's all a matter of what your interests are. Taxonomically speaking, a lobster is a marine crustacean of the family Homaridae, characterized by five pairs of jointed legs, the

---

1   [Wallace's note] There's a comprehensive native apothegm: "Camden by the sea, Rockland by the smell."

2   *Gourmet article* This article originally appeared in *Gourmet* magazine.

3   *Lee Ann Womack* American pop-country musician; *Orleans* American pop-rock band.

4   *Lobster thermidor* French lobster in cream sauce dish requiring extensive preparation.

5   [Wallace's note] N.B. All personally connected parties have made it clear from the start that they do not want to be talked about in this article.

first pair terminating in large pincerish claws used for subduing prey. Like many other species of benthic[1] carnivore, lobsters are both hunters and scavengers. They have stalked eyes, gills on their legs, and antennae. There are a dozen or so different kinds worldwide, of which the relevant species here is the Maine lobster, *Homarus americanus*. The name "lobster" comes from the Old English *loppestre*, which is thought to be a corrupt form of the Latin word for locust combined with the Old English *loppe*, which meant spider.

Moreover, a crustacean is an aquatic arthropod of the class Crustacea, which comprises crabs, shrimp, barnacles, lobsters, and freshwater crayfish. All this is right there in the encyclopedia. And arthropods are members of the phylum Arthropoda, which phylum covers insects, spiders, crustaceans, and centipedes/millipedes, all of whose main commonality, besides the absence of a centralized brain-spine assembly, is a chitinous exoskeleton composed of segments, to which appendages are articulated in pairs.

The point is that lobsters are basically giant sea insects.[2] Like most arthropods, they date from the Jurassic period, biologically so much older than mammalia that they might as well be from another planet. And they are—particularly in their natural brown-green state, brandishing their claws like weapons and with thick antennae awhip—not nice to look at. And it's true that they are garbagemen of the sea, eaters of dead stuff,[3] although they'll also eat some live shellfish, certain kinds of injured fish, and sometimes one another.

But they are themselves good eating. Or so we think now. Up until sometime in the 1800s, though, lobster was literally low-class food, eaten only by the poor and institutionalized. Even in the harsh penal environment of early America, some colonies had laws against feeding lobsters to inmates more than once a week because it was thought to be cruel and unusual, like making people eat rats. One reason for their low status was how plentiful lobsters were in old New England. "Unbelievable abundance" is how one source describes the situation, including accounts of Plymouth Pilgrims wading out and capturing all they wanted by hand, and of early Boston's seashore being littered with lobsters after hard storms—these latter were treated as a smelly nuisance and ground up for fertilizer. There is also the fact that premodern lobster was cooked dead and then preserved, usually packed in salt or crude hermetic containers. Maine's earliest lobster industry was based around a dozen such seaside canneries in the 1840s, from which lobster was shipped as far away as California, in demand only because it was cheap and high in protein, basically chewable fuel.

---

1   *benthic* Bottom-dwelling.

2   [Wallace's note] Midcoasters' native term for a lobster is, in fact, "bug," as in "Come around on Sunday and we'll cook up some bugs."

3   [Wallace's note] Factoid: Lobster traps are usually baited with dead herring.

Now, of course, lobster is posh, a delicacy, only a step or two down from caviar. The meat is richer and more substantial than most fish, its taste subtle compared to the marine-gaminess of mussels and clams. In the US pop-food imagination, lobster is now the seafood analog to steak, with which it's so often twinned as Surf 'n' Turf on the really expensive part of the chain steakhouse menu.

In fact, one obvious project of the MLF, and of its omnipresently sponsorial Maine Lobster Promotion Council, is to counter the idea that lobster is unusually luxe or unhealthy or expensive, suitable only for effete palates or the occasional blow-the-diet treat. It is emphasized over and over in presentations and pamphlets at the festival that lobster meat has fewer calories, less cholesterol, and less saturated fat than chicken.[1] And in the Main Eating Tent, you can get a "quarter" (industry shorthand for a 1¼-pound lobster), a four-ounce cup of melted butter, a bag of chips, and a soft roll w/ butter-pat for around $12.00, which is only slightly more expensive than supper at McDonald's.

Be apprised, though, that the Main Lobster Festival's democratization of lobster comes with all the massed inconvenience and aesthetic compromise of real democracy. See, for example, the aforementioned Main Eating Tent, for which there is a constant Disneyland-grade queue, and which turns out to be a square quarter mile of awning-shaded cafeteria lines and rows of long institutional tables at which friend and stranger alike sit cheek by jowl, cracking and chewing and dribbling. It's hot, and the sagged roof traps the steam and the smells, which latter are strong and only partly food-related. It is also loud, and a good percentage of the total noise is masticatory. The suppers come in styrofoam trays, and the soft drinks are iceless and flat, and the coffee is convenience-store coffee in more styrofoam, and the utensils are plastic (there are none of the special long skinny forks for pushing out the tail meat, though a few savvy diners bring their own). Nor do they give you near enough napkins considering how messy lobster is to eat, especially when you're squeezed onto benches alongside children of various ages and vastly different levels of fine-motor development—not to mention the people who've somehow smuggled in their own beer in enormous aisle-blocking coolers, or who all of a sudden produce their own plastic tablecloths and spread them over large portions of tables to try to reserve them (the tables) for their little groups. And so on. Any one example is no more than a petty inconvenience, of course, but the MLF turns out to be full of irksome little downers like this—see for instance the Main Stage's headliner shows, where it turns out you have to

---

1   [Wallace's note] Of course, the common practice of dipping the lobster meat in melted butter torpedoes all these happy fat-specs, which none of the council's promotional stuff ever mentions, any more than potato industry PR talks about sour cream and bacon bits.

pay $20 extra for a folding chair if you want to sit down; or the North Tent's mad scramble for the Nyquil-cup-sized samples of finalists' entries handed out after the Cooking Competition; or the much-touted Maine Sea Goddess pageant finals, which turn out to be excruciatingly long and to consist mainly of endless thanks and tributes to local sponsors. Let's not even talk about the grossly inadequate Port-A-San facilities or the fact that there's nowhere to wash your hands before or after eating. What the Maine Lobster Festival really is is a midlevel county fair with a culinary hook, and in this respect it's not unlike Tidewater crab festivals, Midwest corn festivals, Texas chili festivals, etc., and shares with these venues the core paradox of all teeming commercial demotic[1] events: It's not for everyone.[2] Nothing against the euphoric senior editor of *Food & Wine*, but I'd be surprised if she'd ever actually been here in Harbor Park, amid crowds of people slapping canal-zone mosquitoes as they eat deep-fried Twinkies and watch Professor Paddywhack, on six-foot stilts

---

1   *demotic* Popular; for the masses.
2   [Wallace's note] In truth, there's a great deal to be said about the differences between working-class Rockland and the heavily populist flavour of its festival versus comfortable and elitist Camden with its expensive view and shops given entirely over to $200 sweaters and great rows of Victorian homes converted to upscale B&Bs. And about these differences as two sides of the great coin that is US tourism. Very little of which will be said here, except to amplify the above-mentioned paradox and to reveal your assigned correspondent's own preferences. I confess that I have never understood why so many people's idea of a fun vacation is to don flip-flops and sunglasses and crawl through maddening traffic to loud, hot, crowded tourist venues in order to sample a "local flavour" that is by definition ruined by the presence of tourists. This may (as my festival companions keep pointing out) all be a matter of personality and hardwired taste: the fact that I do not like tourist venues means that I'll never understand their appeal and so am probably not the one to talk about it (the supposed appeal). But, since this FN will almost surely not survive magazine-editing anyway, here goes:
    As I see it, it probably really is good for the soul to be a tourist, even if it's only once in a while. Not good for the soul in a refreshing or enlivening way, though, but rather in a grim, steely-eyed, let's-look-honestly-at-the-facts-and-find-some-way-to-deal-with-them way. My personal experience has not been that travelling around the country is broadening or relaxing, or that radical changes in place and context have a salutary effect, but rather that intranational tourism is radically constricting, and humbling in the hardest way—hostile to my fantasy of being a true individual, of living somehow outside and above it all. (Coming up is the part that my companions find especially unhappy and repellent, a sure way to spoil the fun of vacation travel:) To be a mass tourist, for me, is to become a pure late-date American: alien, ignorant, greedy for something you cannot ever have, disappointed in a way you can never admit. It is to spoil, by way of sheer ontology, the very unspoiledness you are there to experience. It is to impose yourself on places that in all non-economic ways would be better, realer, without you. It is, in lines and gridlock and transaction after transaction, to confront a dimension of yourself that is as inescapable as it is painful: As a tourist, you become economically significant but existentially loathsome, an insect on a dead thing.

in a raincoat with plastic lobsters protruding from all directions on springs, terrify their children.

Lobster is essentially a summer food. This is because we now prefer our lobsters fresh, which means they have to be recently caught, which for both tactical and economic reasons takes place at depths less than 25 fathoms. Lobsters tend to be hungriest and most active (i.e., most trappable) at summer water temperatures of 45–50 degrees. In the autumn, most Maine lobsters migrate out into deeper water, either for warmth or to avoid the heavy waves that pound New England's coast all winter. Some burrow into the bottom. They might hibernate; nobody's sure. Summer is also lobsters' molting season— specifically early- to mid-July. Chitinous arthropods grow by molting, rather the way people have to buy bigger clothes as they age and gain weight. Since lobsters can live to be over 100, they can also get to be quite large, as in 30 pounds or more—though truly senior lobsters are rare now, because New England's waters are so heavily trapped.[1] Anyway, hence the culinary distinction between hard- and soft-shell lobsters, the latter sometimes a.k.a. shedders. A soft-shell lobster is one that has recently molted. In midcoast restaurants, the summer menu often offers both kinds, with shedders being slightly cheaper even though they're easier to dismantle and the meat is allegedly sweeter. The reason for the discount is that a molting lobster uses a layer of seawater for insulation while its new shell is hardening, so there's slightly less actual meat when you crack open a shedder, plus a redolent gout of water that gets all over everything and can sometimes jet out lemonlike and catch a tablemate right in the eye. If it's winter or you're buying lobster someplace far from New England, on the other hand, you can almost bet that the lobster is a hard-shell, which for obvious reasons travel better.

As an à la carte entrée, lobster can be baked, broiled, steamed, grilled, sautéed, stir-fried, or microwaved. The most common method, though, is boiling. If you're someone who enjoys having lobster at home, this is probably the way you do it, since boiling is so easy. You need a large kettle w/ cover, which you fill about half full with water (the standard advice is that you want 2.5 quarts of water per lobster). Seawater is optimal, or you can add two tbsp salt per quart from the tap. It also helps to know how much your lobsters weigh. You get the water boiling, put in the lobsters one at a time, cover the kettle, and bring it back up to a boil. Then you bank the heat and let the kettle simmer—ten minutes for the first pound of lobster, then three minutes for each pound after that. (This is assuming you've got hard-shell lobsters, which,

---

1   [Wallace's note] Datum: In a good year, the US industry produces around 80,000,000 pounds of lobster, and Maine accounts for more than half that total.

again, if you don't live between Boston and Halifax is probably what you've got. For shedders, you're supposed to subtract three minutes from the total.) The reason the kettle's lobsters turn scarlet is that boiling somehow suppresses every pigment in their chitin but one. If you want an easy test of whether the lobsters are done, you try pulling on one of their antennae—if it comes out of the head with minimal effort, you're ready to eat.

A detail so obvious that most recipes don't even bother to mention it is that each lobster is supposed to be alive when you put it in the kettle. This is part of lobster's modern appeal—it's the freshest food there is. There's no decomposition between harvesting and eating. And not only do lobsters require no cleaning or dressing or plucking, they're relatively easy for vendors to keep alive. They come up alive in the traps, are placed in containers of seawater, and can—so long as the water's aerated and the animals' claws are pegged or banded to keep them from tearing one another up under the stresses of captivity[1]—survive right up until they're boiled. Most of us have been in supermarkets or restaurants that feature tanks of live lobsters, from which you can pick out your supper while it watches you point. And part of the overall spectacle of the Maine Lobster Festival is that you can see actual lobstermen's vessels docking at the wharves along the northeast grounds and unloading fresh-caught product, which is transferred by hand or cart 150 yards to the great clear tanks stacked up around the festival's cooker—which is, as mentioned, billed as the World's Largest Lobster Cooker and can process over 100 lobsters at a time for the Main Eating Tent.

So then here is a question that's all but unavoidable at the World's Largest Lobster Cooker, and may arise in kitchens across the US: Is it all right to boil a sentient creature alive just for our gustatory[2] pleasure? A related set of concerns: Is the previous question irksomely PC or sentimental? What does "all right" even mean in this context? Is the whole thing just a matter of personal choice?

---

1   [Wallace's note] N.B. Similar reasoning underlies the practice of what's termed "debeaking" broiler chickens and brood hens in modern factory farms. Maximum commercial efficiency requires that enormous poultry populations be confined in unnaturally close quarters, under which conditions many birds go crazy and peck one another to death. As a purely observational side-note, be apprised that debeaking is usually an automated process and that the chickens receive no anaesthetic. It's not clear to me whether most *Gourmet* readers know about debeaking, or about related practices like dehorning cattle in commercial feed lots, cropping swine's tails in factory hog farms to keep psychotically bored neighbours from chewing them off, and so forth. It so happens that your assigned correspondent knew almost nothing about standard meat-industry operations before starting work on this article.

2   *gustatory* Taste-related.

As you may or may not know, a certain well-known group called People for the Ethical Treatment of Animals thinks that the morality of lobster-boiling is not just a matter of individual conscience. In fact, one of the very first things we hear about the MLF ... well, to set the scene: We're coming in by cab from the almost indescribably odd and rustic Knox County Airport[1] very late on the night before the festival opens, sharing the cab with a wealthy political consultant who lives on Vinalhaven Island in the bay half the year (he's headed for the island ferry in Rockland). The consultant and cabdriver are responding to informal journalistic probes about how people who live in the midcoast region actually view the MLF, as in is the festival just a big-dollar tourist thing or is it something local residents look forward to attending, take genuine civic pride in, etc. The cabdriver (who's in his seventies, one of apparently a whole platoon of retirees the cab company puts on to help with the summer rush, and wears a US-flag lapel pin, and drives in what can only be called a very *deliberate* way) assures us that locals do endorse and enjoy the MLF, although he himself hasn't gone in years, and now come to think of it no one he and his wife know has, either. However, the demilocal consultant's been to recent festivals a couple times (one gets the impression it was at his wife's behest), of which his most vivid impression was that "you have to line up for an ungodly long time to get your lobsters, and meanwhile there are all these ex–flower children coming up and down along the line handing out pamphlets that say the lobsters die in terrible pain and you shouldn't eat them."

And it turns out that the post-hippies of the consultant's recollection were activists from PETA. There were no PETA people in obvious view at the 2003 MLF,[2] but they've been conspicuous at many of the recent festi-

---

1   [Wallace's note] The terminal used to be somebody's house, for example, and the lost-luggage-reporting room was clearly once a pantry.

2   [Wallace's note] It turned out that one Mr. William R. Rivas-Rivas, a high-ranking PETA official out of the group's Virginia headquarters, was indeed there this year, albeit solo, working the festival's main and side entrances on Saturday, 2 August, handing out pamphlets and adhesive stickers emblazoned with "Being Boiled Hurts," which is the tagline in most of PETA's published material about lobsters. I learned that he'd been there only later, when speaking with Mr. Rivas-Rivas on the phone. I'm not sure how we missed seeing him *in situ* at the festival, and I can't see much to do except apologize for the oversight—although it's also true that Saturday was the day of the big MLF parade through Rockland, which basic journalistic responsibility seemed to require going to (and which, with all due respect, meant that Saturday was maybe not the best day for PETA to work the Harbor Park grounds, especially if it was going to be just one person for one day, since a lot of diehard MLF partisans were off-site watching the parade (which, again with no offence intended, was in truth kind of cheesy and boring, consisting mostly of slow home-made floats and various midcoast people waving at one another, and with an extremely annoying man dressed as Blackbeard ranging up and down the length of the crowd saying "Arrr" over and over and brandishing a plastic sword at people, etc.; plus it rained)).

vals. Since at least the mid-1990s, articles in everything from *The Camden Herald* to *The New York Times* have described PETA urging boycotts of the Maine Lobster Festival, often deploying celebrity spokesmen like Mary Tyler Moore for open letters and ads saying stuff like "Lobsters are extraordinarily sensitive" and "To me, eating a lobster is out of the question." More concrete is the oral testimony of Dick, our florid and extremely gregarious rental-car liaison,[1] to the effect that PETA's been around so much during recent years that a kind of brittlely tolerant homeostasis[2] now obtains between the activists and the festival's locals, e.g.: "We had some incidents a couple years ago. One lady took most of her clothes off and painted herself like a lobster, almost got herself arrested. But for the most part they're let alone. [Rapid series of small ambiguous laughs, which with Dick happens a lot.] They do their thing and we do our thing."

This whole interchange takes place on Route 1, 30 July, during a four-mile, 50-minute ride from the airport[3] to the dealership to sign car-rental papers. Several irreproducible segues down the road from the PETA anecdotes, Dick—whose son-in-law happens to be a professional lobsterman and one of the Main Eating Tent's regular suppliers—explains what he and his family feel is the crucial mitigating factor in the whole morality-of-boiling-lobsters-alive issue: "There's a part of the brain in people and animals that lets us feel pain, and lobsters' brains don't have this part."

Besides the fact that it's incorrect in about nine different ways, the main reason Dick's statement is interesting is that its thesis is more or less echoed by the festival's own pronouncement on lobsters and pain, which is part of a Test Your Lobster IQ quiz that appears in the 2003 MLF program courtesy of the Maine Lobster Promotion Council:

> The nervous system of a lobster is very simple, and is in fact most similar to the nervous system of the grasshopper. It is decentralized with no brain. There is no cerebral cortex, which in humans is the area of the brain that gives the experience of pain.

---

1 [Wallace's note] By profession, Dick is actually a car salesman; the midcoast region's National Car Rental franchise operates out of a Chevy dealership in Thomaston.

2 *homeostasis* I.e., balance.

3 [Wallace's note] The short version regarding why we were back at the airport after already arriving the previous night involves lost luggage and a miscommunication about where and what the midcoast's National franchise was—Dick came out personally to the airport and got us, out of no evident motive but kindness. (He also talked nonstop the entire way, with a very distinctive speaking style that can be described only as manically laconic; the truth is that I now know more about this man than I do about some members of my own family.)

Though it sounds more sophisticated, a lot of the neurology in this latter claim is still either false or fuzzy. The human cerebral cortex is the brain-part that deals with higher faculties like reason, metaphysical self-awareness, language, etc. Pain reception is known to be part of a much older and more primitive system of nociceptors and prostaglandins that are managed by the brain stem and thalamus.[1, 2] On the other hand, it is true that the cerebral cortex is involved in what's variously called suffering, distress, or the emotional experience of pain—i.e., experiencing painful stimuli as unpleasant, very unpleasant, unbearable, and so on.

Before we go any further, let's acknowledge that the questions of whether and how different kinds of animals feel pain, and of whether and why it might be justifiable to inflict pain on them in order to eat them, turn out to be extremely complex and difficult. And comparative neuroanatomy is only part of the problem. Since pain is a totally subjective mental experience, we do not have direct access to anyone or anything's pain but our own; and even just the principles by which we can infer that other human beings experience pain and have a legitimate interest in not feeling pain involve hard-core philosophy—metaphysics, epistemology, value theory, ethics. The fact that even the most highly evolved nonhuman mammals can't use language to communicate with us about their subjective mental experience is only the first layer of additional complication in trying to extend our reasoning about pain and morality to animals. And everything gets progressively more abstract and convoluted as we move farther and farther out from the higher-type mammals into cattle and swine and dogs and cats and rodents, and then birds and fish, and finally invertebrates like lobsters.

The more important point here, though, is that the whole animal-cruelty-and-eating issue is not just complex, it's also uncomfortable. It is, at any rate, uncomfortable for me, and for just about everyone I know who enjoys a variety of foods and yet does not want to see herself as cruel or unfeeling. As far as I can tell, my own main way of dealing with this conflict has been to avoid thinking about the whole unpleasant thing. I should add that it appears to me unlikely that many readers of *Gourmet* wish to think about it, either, or to be queried about the morality of their eating habits in the pages of a culinary monthly. Since, however, the assigned subject of this

---

1   *prostaglandins* Chemicals similar to hormones; *thalamus* Part of the brain that transmits sensory input to the cerebral cortex.

2   [Wallace's note] To elaborate by way of example: The common experience of accidentally touching a hot stove and yanking your hand back before you're even aware that anything's going on is explained by the fact that many of the processes by which we detect and avoid painful stimuli do not involve the cortex. In the case of the hand and stove, the brain is bypassed altogether; all the important neurochemical action takes place in the spine.

article is what it was like to attend the 2003 MLF, and thus to spend several days in the midst of a great mass of Americans all eating lobster, and thus to be more or less impelled to think hard about lobster and the experience of buying and eating lobster, it turns out that there is no honest way to avoid certain moral questions.

There are several reasons for this. For one thing, it's not just that lobsters get boiled alive, it's that you do it yourself—or at least it's done specifically for you, on-site.[1] As mentioned, the World's Largest Lobster Cooker, which is highlighted as an attraction in the festival's program, is right out there on the MLF's north grounds for everyone to see. Try to imagine a Nebraska Beef Festival[2] at which part of the festivities is watching trucks pull up and the live cattle get driven down the ramp and slaughtered right there on the World's Largest Killing Floor or something—there's no way.

The intimacy of the whole thing is maximized at home, which of course is where most lobster gets prepared and eaten (although note already the semi-conscious euphemism "prepared," which in the case of lobsters really means killing them right there in our kitchens). The basic scenario is that we come in from the store and make our little preparations like getting the kettle filled and boiling, and then we lift the lobsters out of the bag or whatever retail container they came home in … whereupon some uncomfortable things start to happen. However stuporous a lobster is from the trip home, for instance, it tends to come alarmingly to life when placed in boiling water. If you're tilting it from a container into the steaming kettle, the lobster will sometimes try to cling to the container's sides or even to hook its claws over the kettle's rim like

---

1 [Wallace's note] Morality-wise, let's concede that this cuts both ways. Lobster-eating is at least not abetted by the system of corporate factory farms that produces most beef, pork, and chicken. Because, if nothing else, of the way they're marketed and packaged for sale, we eat these latter meats without having to consider that they were once conscious, sentient creatures to whom horrible things were done. (N.B. "Horrible" here meaning really, really horrible. Write off to PETA or peta.org for their free "Meet Your Meat" video, narrated by Mr. Alec Baldwin, if you want to see just about everything meat-related you don't want to see or think about. (N.B.$_2$ Not that PETA's any sort of font of unspun truth. Like many partisans in complex moral disputes, the PETA people are fanatics, and a lot of their rhetoric seems simplistic and self-righteous. But this particular video, replete with actual factory-farm and corporate-slaughterhouse footage, is both credible and traumatizing.))

2 [Wallace's note] Is it significant that "lobster," "fish," and "chicken" are our culture's words for both the animal and the meat, whereas most mammals seem to require euphemisms like "beef" and "pork" that help us separate the meat we eat from the living creature the meat once was? Is this evidence that some kind of deep unease about eating higher animals is endemic enough to show up in English usage, but that the unease diminishes as we move out of the mammalian order? (And is "lamb"/"lamb" the counterexample that sinks the whole theory, or are there special, biblico-historical reasons for that equivalence?)

a person trying to keep from going over the edge of a roof. And worse is when the lobster's fully immersed. Even if you cover the kettle and turn away, you can usually hear the cover rattling and clanking as the lobster tries to push it off. Or the creature's claws scraping the sides of the kettle as it thrashes around. The lobster, in other words, behaves very much as you or I would behave if we were plunged into boiling water (with the obvious exception of screaming).[1] A blunter way to say this is that the lobster acts as if it's in terrible pain, caus-ing some cooks to leave the kitchen altogether and to take one of those little lightweight plastic oven-timers with them into another room and wait until the whole process is over.

There happen to be two main criteria that most ethicists agree on for deter-mining whether a living creature has the capacity to suffer and so has genuine interests that it may or may not be our moral duty to consider.[2] One is how much of the neurological hardware required for pain-experience the animal comes equipped with—nociceptors, prostaglandins, neuronal opioid[3] recep-tors, etc. The other criterion is whether the animal demonstrates behaviour associated with pain. And it takes a lot of intellectual gymnastics and behav-iourist hairsplitting not to see struggling, thrashing, and lid-clattering as just such pain-behaviour. According to marine zoologists, it usually takes lobsters between 35 and 45 seconds to die in boiling water. (No source I could find talked about how long it takes them to die in superheated steam; one rather hopes it's faster.)

There are, of course, other fairly common ways to kill your lobster on-site and so achieve maximum freshness. Some cooks' practice is to drive a sharp

---

1   [Wallace's note] There's a relevant populist myth about the high-pitched whistling sound that sometimes issues from a pot of boiling lobster. The sound is really vented steam from the layer of seawater between the lobster's flesh and its carapace (this is why shedders whistle more than hard-shells), but the pop version has it that the sound is the lobster's rabbit-like death-scream. Lobsters communicate via pheromones in their urine and don't have anything close to the vocal equipment for screaming, but the myth's very persis-tent—which might, once again, point to a low-level cultural unease about the boiling thing.

2   [Wallace's note] "Interests" basically means strong and legitimate preferences, which obviously require some degree of consciousness, responsiveness to stimuli, etc. See, for instance, the utilitarian philosopher Peter Singer, whose 1974 *Animal Liberation* is more or less the bible of the modern animal-rights movement:

   It would be nonsense to say that it was not in the interests of a stone to be kicked along the road by a schoolboy. A stone does not have interests because it cannot suf-fer. Nothing that we can do to it could possibly make any difference to its welfare. A mouse, on the other hand, does have an interest in not being kicked along the road, because it will suffer if it is.

3   *opioid* Brain chemical that reduces pain.

heavy knife point-first into a spot just above the midpoint between the lobster's eyestalks (more or less where the Third Eye is in human foreheads). This is alleged either to kill the lobster instantly or to render it insensate, and is said at least to eliminate some of the cowardice involved in throwing a creature into boiling water and then fleeing the room. As far as I can tell from talking to proponents of the knife-in-the-head method, the idea is that it's more violent but ultimately more merciful, plus that a willingness to exert personal agency and accept responsibility for stabbing the lobster's head honours the lobster somehow and entitles one to eat it (there's often a vague sort of Native American spirituality-of-the-hunt flavour to pro-knife arguments). But the problem with the knife method is basic biology: Lobsters' nervous systems operate off not one but several ganglia, a.k.a. nerve bundles, which are sort of wired in series and distributed all along the lobster's underside, from stem to stern. And disabling only the frontal ganglion does not normally result in quick death or unconsciousness.

Another alternative is to put the lobster in cold saltwater and then very slowly bring it up to a full boil. Cooks who advocate this method are going on the analogy to a frog, which can supposedly be kept from jumping out of a boiling pot by heating the water incrementally. In order to save a lot of research-summarizing, I'll simply assure you that the analogy between frogs and lobsters turns out not to hold—plus, if the kettle's water isn't aerated seawater, the immersed lobster suffers from slow suffocation, although usually not decisive enough suffocation to keep it from still thrashing and clattering when the water gets hot enough to kill it. In fact, lobsters boiled incrementally often display a whole bonus set of gruesome, convulsionlike reactions that you don't see in regular boiling.

Ultimately, the only certain virtues of the home-lobotomy and slow-heating methods are comparative, because there are even worse/crueler ways people prepare lobster. Time-thrifty cooks sometimes microwave them alive (usually after poking several extra vent-holes in the carapace, which is a precaution most shellfish-microwavers learn about the hard way). Live dismemberment, on the other hand, is big in Europe—some chefs cut the lobster in half before cooking; others like to tear off the claws and tail and toss only these parts in the pot.

And there's more unhappy news respecting suffering-criterion number one. Lobsters don't have much in the way of eyesight or hearing, but they do have an exquisite tactile sense, one facilitated by hundreds of thousands of tiny hairs that protrude through their carapace. "Thus it is," in the words of T.M. Prudden's industry classic *About Lobster*, "that although encased in what seems a solid, impenetrable armor, the lobster can receive stimuli and impressions from without as readily as if it possessed a soft and delicate skin." And lobsters do have nociceptors,[1] as well as invertebrate versions of the prostaglandins and major neurotransmitters via which our own brains register pain.

Lobsters do not, on the other hand, appear to have the equipment for making or absorbing natural opioids like endorphins and enkephalins, which are what more advanced nervous systems use to try to handle intense pain. From this fact, though, one could conclude either that lobsters are maybe even *more* vulnerable to pain, since they lack mammalian nervous systems' built-in analgesia,[2] or, instead, that the absence of natural opioids implies an absence of the really intense pain-sensations that natural opioids are designed to mitigate. I for one can detect a marked upswing in mood as I contemplate this latter possibility. It could be that their lack of endorphin/enkephalin hardware means that lobsters' raw subjective experience of pain is so radically different from mammals' that it may not even deserve the term "pain." Perhaps lobsters are more like those frontal-lobotomy patients one reads about who report experiencing pain in a totally different way than you and I. These patients evidently do feel physical pain, neurologically speaking, but don't dislike it—though neither do they like it; it's more that they feel it but don't feel anything *about* it—the point being that the pain is not distressing to them or something they want to get away from. Maybe lobsters, who are also without frontal lobes, are detached from the neurological-registration-of-injury-or-hazard we call pain in just the same way. There is, after all, a difference between (1) pain as a purely neurological event, and (2) actual suffering, which seems crucially to involve an emotional component, an awareness of pain as unpleasant, as something to fear/dislike/want to avoid.

Still, after all the abstract intellection, there remain the facts of the frantically clanking lid, the pathetic clinging to the edge of the pot. Standing at the stove, it is hard to deny in any meaningful way that this is a living creature experiencing pain and wishing to avoid/escape the painful experience. To my lay mind, the lobster's behaviour in the kettle appears to be the expression of a *preference*; and it may well be that an ability to form preferences is the decisive criterion for real suffering.[3] The logic of this (preference → suffering) relation may be easiest to see in the negative case. If you cut certain kinds of worms in half, the halves will often keep crawling around and going about

---

1   [Wallace's note] This is the neurological term for special pain-receptors that are "sensitive to potentially damaging extremes of temperature, to mechanical forces, and to chemical substances which are released when body tissues are damaged."

2   *analgesia* Pain reduction.

3   [Wallace's note] "Preference" is maybe roughly synonymous with "interests," but it is a better term for our purposes because it's less abstractly philosophical—"preference" seems more personal, and it's the whole idea of a living creature's personal experience that's at issue.

their vermiform business as if nothing had happened. When we assert, based on their post-op behaviour, that these worms appear not to be suffering, what we're really saying is that there's no sign that the worms know anything bad has happened or would *prefer* not to have gotten cut in half.

Lobsters, though, are known to exhibit preferences. Experiments have shown that they can detect changes of only a degree or two in water temperature; one reason for their complex migratory cycles (which can often cover 100-plus miles a year) is to pursue the temperatures they like best.[1] And, as mentioned, they're bottom-dwellers and do not like bright light—if a tank of food lobsters is out in the sunlight or a store's fluorescence, the lobsters will always congregate in whatever part is darkest. Fairly solitary in the ocean, they also clearly dislike the crowding that's part of their captivity in tanks, since (as also mentioned) one reason why lobsters' claws are banded on capture is to keep them from attacking one another under the stress of close-quarter storage.

In any event, at the MLF, standing by the bubbling tanks outside the World's Largest Lobster Cooker, watching the fresh-caught lobsters pile over one another, wave their hobbled claws impotently, huddle in the rear corners, or scrabble frantically back from the glass as you approach, it is difficult not to sense that they're unhappy, or frightened, even if it's some rudimentary version of these feelings ... and, again, why does rudimentariness even enter into it? Why is a primitive, inarticulate form of suffering less urgent or uncomfortable for the person who's helping to inflict it by paying for the food it results in? I'm

---

1   [Wallace's note] Of course, the most common sort of counterargument here would begin by objecting that "like best" is really just a metaphor, and a misleadingly anthropomorphic one at that. The counterarguer would posit that the lobster seeks to maintain a certain optimal ambient temperature out of nothing but unconscious instinct (with a similar explanation for the low-light affinities upcoming in the main text). The thrust of such a counterargument will be that the lobster's thrashings and clankings in the kettle express not unpreferred pain but involuntary reflexes, like your leg shooting out when the doctor hits your knee. Be advised that there are professional scientists, including many researchers who use animals in experiments, who hold to the view that nonhuman creatures have no real feelings at all, merely "behaviours." Be further advised that this view has a long history that goes all the way back to Descartes, although its modern support comes mostly from behaviourist psychology. [René Descartes (1596–1650) was an influential French philosopher; behaviourist psychology interprets psychology exclusively in terms of behaviour as opposed to internal mental states.]

    To these what-looks-like-pain-is-really-just-reflexes counterarguments, however, there happen to be all sorts of scientific and pro-animal-rights counter-counterarguments. And then further attempted rebuttals and redirects, and so on. Suffice to say that both the scientific and the philosophical arguments on either side of the animal-suffering issue are involved, abstruse, technical, often informed by self-interest or ideology, and in the end so totally inconclusive that as a practical matter, in the kitchen or restaurant, it all still seems to come down to individual conscience, going with (no pun) your gut.

not trying to give you a PETA-like screed here—at least I don't think so. I'm trying, rather, to work out and articulate some of the troubling questions that arise amid all the laughter and saltation[1] and community pride of the Maine Lobster Festival. The truth is that if you, the festival attendee, permit yourself to think that lobsters can suffer and would rather not, the MLF begins to take on the aspect of something like a Roman circus or medieval torture-fest.

Does that comparison seem a bit much? If so, exactly why? Or what about this one: Is it possible that future generations will regard our own present agribusiness and eating practices in much the same way we now view Nero's entertainments or Mengele's experiments?[2] My own immediate reaction is that such a comparison is hysterical, extreme—and yet the reason it seems extreme to me appears to be that I believe animals are less morally important than human beings;[3] and when it comes to defending such a belief, even to myself, I have to acknowledge that (a) I have an obvious selfish interest in this belief, since I like to eat certain kinds of animals and want to be able to keep doing it, and (b) I haven't succeeded in working out any sort of personal ethical system in which the belief is truly defensible instead of just selfishly convenient.

Given this article's venue and my own lack of culinary sophistication, I'm curious about whether the reader can identify with any of these reactions and acknowledgements and discomforts. I am also concerned not to come off as shrill or preachy when what I really am is more like confused. For those *Gourmet* readers who enjoy well-prepared and -presented meals involving beef, veal, lamb, pork, chicken, lobster, etc.: Do you think much about the (possible) moral status and (probable) suffering of the animals involved? If you do, what ethical convictions have you worked out that permit you not just to eat but to savour and enjoy flesh-based viands[4] (since of course refined *enjoyment*, rather than mere ingestion, is the whole point of gastronomy)? If, on the other hand, you'll have no truck with confusions or convictions and regard stuff like the previous paragraph as just so much fatuous navel-gazing, what makes it feel truly okay, inside, to just dismiss the whole issue out of hand? That is, is your refusal to think about any of this the product of actual thought, or is it

---

1   *saltation* I.e., dancing, jumping around.

2   *Nero's entertainments* Among the spectacles that Roman Emperor Nero (37–68 CE) staged for his people's enjoyment were gladiator battles and the brutal public execution of Christians; *Mengele's experiments* Nazi doctor Josef Mengele (1911–79) conducted cruel medical experiments on inmates at the Auschwitz concentration camp.

3   [Wallace's note] Meaning a *lot* less important, apparently, since the moral comparison here is not the value of one human's life vs. the value of one animal's life, but rather the value of one animal's life vs. the value of one human's taste for a particular kind of protein. Even the most diehard carniphile will acknowledge that it's possible to live and eat well without consuming animals.

4   *viands* Foods.

just that you don't want to think about it? And if the latter, then why not? Do you ever think, even idly, about the possible reasons for your reluctance to think about it? I am not trying to bait anyone here—I'm genuinely curious. After all, isn't being extra aware and attentive and thoughtful about one's food and its overall context part ·of what distinguishes a real gourmet? Or is all the gourmet's extra attention and sensibility just supposed to be sensuous? Is it really all just a matter of taste and presentation?

These last few queries, though, while sincere, obviously involve much larger and more abstract questions about the connections (if any) between aesthetics and morality—about what the adjective in a phrase like "The Magazine of Good Living"[1] is really supposed to mean—and these questions lead straightaway into such deep and treacherous waters that it's probably best to stop the public discussion right here. There are limits to what even interested persons can ask of each other.

—2004

---

1   *The Magazine ... Living* Slogan of *Gourmet* magazine.

Miriam Toews
b. 1964

"This town is so severe. And silent. It makes me crazy, the silence." So the teenaged Nomi Nickel describes her home town, the Mennonite community of East Village, in Miriam Toews's fourth novel, *A Complicated Kindness* (2004). That book, which was a best-seller and winner of the Governor General's Award, established Toews as a major figure on the Canadian literary landscape. Like most of her other work, it draws powerfully upon Toews's experience growing up in the town of Steinbach, Manitoba. In Toews's fiction the currents of comedy are often as powerful as those of sadness or despair—and both often spring from her religious upbringing. "We're Mennonites," Nomi tells the reader: "As far as I know, we are the most embarrassing sub-sect of people to belong to if you're a teenager."

Toews is known for her sure touch with wry comedy, but her life and her work have also been touched by tragedy. In 1998, Toews's father committed suicide after a lifelong battle with bipolar disorder. Toews paid tribute to him in an essay on the connections between his Mennonite beliefs and his struggles with depression; "A Father's Faith" (1999) was first published in a magazine, and later reprinted in an anthology of women's writing, *Dropped Threads* (2001). Her full-length memoir, *Swing Low: A Life* (2000), was told from the point of view of her father. Her 2008 novel, *The Flying Troutmans*, also centres on mental illness. It tells the story of narrator Hattie's road trip with her niece and nephew, whose mother (Hattie's sister) suffers from severe depression.

In 2007 Toews was asked to star in Mexican director Carlo Reygadas' *Silent Light* (2007), a film set in a Mennonite community in Northern Mexico. Toews drew on that experience for her 2011 novel, *Irma Voth*, which concerns two young women whose family has moved from the Canadian prairie to a Mennonite community in Mexico; the arrival of a film crew who plan to make a film about the community becomes the catalyst for change.

In describing what she writes about, Toews has sometimes emphasized simple contrasts. In a 2008 interview with *Quill & Quire*, for example, she summed things up in this way: "Life is funny and life is sad. Life is comic and life is tragic. It's a breeze and it's hell." In "A Father's Faith," though—as in the best of her fiction—the interest comes less from simple oppositions than from Toews's sure feel for complications and for subtleties.

A Father's Faith

On the morning on May 13, 1998, my father woke up, had breakfast, got dressed and walked away from the Steinbach Bethesda Hospital, where he had been a patient for two and a half weeks. He walked through his beloved hometown, along Hespeler Road, past the old farmhouse where his mother had lived with her second husband, past the water tower, greeting folks in his loud, friendly voice, wishing them well. He passed the site on First Street where the house in which my sister and I grew up once stood. He walked down Main Street, past the Mennonite church where, throughout his life, he had received countless certificates for perfect attendance, past Elmdale School where he had taught grade six for forty years.

As he walked by his home on Brandt Road, he saw his old neighbour Bill sitting in his lawn chair. He waved and smiled again, then he continued on past the cemetery where his parents were buried, and the high school his daughters had attended, and down Highway 52, out of town, past the Frantz Motor Inn, which is just outside the town limits because it serves alcohol and Steinbach is a dry town. He kept walking until he got too tired, so he hitched a ride with a couple of guys who were on their way to buy a fishing licence in the small village of Woodridge on the edge of the Sandilands Forest.

The sun would have been very warm by the time they dropped him off, and he would have taken off his stylish cap and wiped his brow with the back of his hand. I'm sure he thanked them profusely, perhaps offering them ten dollars for their trouble, and then he walked the short distance to the café near the railroad tracks, the place he and my mom would sometimes go for a quiet coffee and a change of scenery. He would have been able to smell the clover growing in the ditches beside the tracks and between the ties. He may have looked down the line and remembered that the train would be coming from Ontario, through Warroad, Minnesota, on its way to Winnipeg.

A beautiful young woman named Stephanie was just beginning her shift and she spoke to him through the screen door at the side of the restaurant. Yes, she said, the train will be here soon. And my dad smiled and thanked her, and mentioned that he could hear the whistle. Moments later, he was dead.

Steinbach is an easy forty-minute drive from Winnipeg, east on the Trans-Canada, then south on Highway 12. On the way into town there's a sign proclaiming "Jesus Saves." On the way back to the city just off Highway 12 there's another that says, "Satan is Real. You Can't Be Neutral. Choose Now." The town has recently become a city of 8,500 people, two-thirds of whom are Mennonite, so it's not surprising that about half of the twenty-four churches are Mennonite and conservative. There is a Catholic church too, but it's new and I'm not sure exactly where it is. A little way down from the bowling alley

I can still make out my name on the sidewalk, carved in big bold letters when I was ten and marking my territory.

My town made sense to me then. For me it was a giant playground where my friends and I roamed freely, using the entire town in a game of arrows—something like hide-and-seek—for which my dad, the teacher, provided boxes and boxes of fresh new chalk and invaluable tips. He had, after all, played the same game in the same town many years before.

At six p.m. the siren would go off at the firehall, reminding all the kids to go home for supper, and at nine p.m. it was set off again, reminding us to go home to bed. I had no worries, and no desire ever to leave this place where everyone knew me. If they couldn't remember my name, they knew I was the younger daughter of Mel and Elvira Toews, granddaughter of C.T. Loewen and Henry Toews, from the Kleine Gemeinde congregation, and so on and so on. All the kids in town, other than the church-sponsored Laotians who came over in the seventies, could be traced all the way back to the precise Russian veldt their great-grandparents had emigrated from. They were some of the thousands of Mennonites who came to Manitoba in the late 1800s to escape religious persecution. They were given free land and a promise that they could, essentially, do their own thing without interference. They wanted to keep the world away from their children and their children away from the world. Naturally it was an impossible ideal.

As I grew older, I became suspicious and critical and restless and angry. Every night I plotted my escape. I imagined that Barkman's giant feed mill on Main Street, partially visible from my bedroom window, was a tall ship that would take me away some day. I looked up places like Hollywood and Manhattan and Venice and Montreal in my Childcraft encyclopedias. I begged my sister to play, over and over, the sad songs from her Jacques Brel piano book, and I'd light candles and sing along, wearing a Pioneer Girls tam[1] on my head, using a chopstick as a cigarette holder, pretending I was Jackie Brel, Jacques's long-lost but just as world-weary Mennonite twin. I couldn't believe that I was stuck in a town like Steinbach, where dancing was a sin and serving beer a felony.

There were other things I became aware of as well. That my grandmother was a vanilla alcoholic who believed she was a teetotaller. That seventy-five-year-old women who had borne thirteen children weren't allowed to speak to the church congregation, but that fifteen-year-old boys were. That every family had a secret. And I learned that my dad had been depressed all his life.

---

1   *Jacques Brel* Belgian singer-songwriter (1929–78) who became famous performing his poetic ballads in Paris clubs; *tam* Scottish soft hat similar to a beret.

I had wondered, when I was a kid, why he spent so much of the weekend in bed and why he didn't talk much at home. Occasionally he'd tell me, sometimes in tears, that he loved me very much and that he wished he were a better father, that he were more involved in my life. But I never felt the need for an apology. It made me happy and a bit envious to know that my dad's students were able to witness his humour and intelligence firsthand, to hear him expound on his favourite subjects: Canadian history, Canadian politics and Canadian newspapers. I remember watching him at work and marvelling at his energy and enthusiasm. I thought he looked very handsome when he rolled up his sleeves and tucked his tie in between the buttons of his shirt, his hands on his hips, all ready for business and hard work.

Teaching school—helping others make sense of the world—was a good profession for a man who was continuously struggling to find meaning in life. I think he needed his students as much as they needed him. By fulfilling his duties, he was also shoring up a psyche at risk of erosion.

Four years before his death he was forced to retire from teaching because of a heart attack and some small strokes. He managed to finish the book he was writing on Canada's prime ministers, but then he seemed to fade away. He spent more and more of his time in bed, in the dark, not getting up even to eat or wash, not interested in watching TV or listening to the radio. Despite our pleading and cajoling, despite the medication and visits to various doctors' offices, appointments he dutifully kept, and despite my mother's unwavering love, we felt we were losing him.

I know about brain chemistry and depression, but there's still a part of me that blames my dad's death on being Mennonite and living in that freaky, austere place where this world isn't good enough and admission into the next one, the perfect one, means everything, where every word and deed gets you closer to or farther away from eternal life. If you don't believe that then nothing Steinbach stands for will make sense. And if life doesn't make sense you lose yourself in it, your spirit decays. That's what I believed had happened to my dad, and that's why I hated my town.

In the weeks and months after his death, my mom and my sister and I tried to piece things together. William Ashdown, the executive director of the Mood Disorders Association of Manitoba, told us the number of mentally ill Mennonites is abnormally high. "We don't know if it's genetic or cultural," he said, "but the Steinbach area is one that we're vitally concerned about."

"It's the way the church delivers the message," says a Mennonite friend of mine, "the message of sin and accountability. To be human, basically, is to be a sinner. So a person, a real believer, starts to get down on himself, and where does it end? They say self-loathing is the cornerstone of depression, right?"

Years ago, the Mennonite Church practised something called "shunning," whereby if you were to leave your husband, or marry outside the Church, or elope, or drink, or in some way contravene the Church's laws or act "out of faith," you could be expelled from the Church and ignored, shunned by the entire community, including your own family. Depression or despair, as it would have been referred to then, was considered to be the result of a lack of faith and therefore could be another reason for shunning.

These days most Mennonites don't officially practise shunning, although William Ashdown claims there are still Mennonites from extreme conservative sects who are being shunned and shamed into silence within their communities for being mentally ill. Certainly Arden Thiessen, the minister of my dad's church, and a long-time friend of his, is aware of the causes of depression and the pain experienced by those who suffer from it. He doesn't see it as a lack of faith, but as an awful sickness.

But I can't help thinking that that history had just a little to do with my alcoholic grandmother's insisting that she was a non-drinker, and my dad's telling his doctors, smiling that beautiful smile of his, that he was fine, just fine.

Not long before he died my dad told me about the time he was five and was having his tonsils out. Just before the operation began he was knocked out with ether and he had a dream that he was somersaulting through the hospital walls, right through, easily, he said, moving his hands in circles through the air. It was wonderful. He told me he would never forget that feeling.

But mostly, the world was a sad and unsafe place for him, and his town provided shelter from it. Maybe he saw this as a gift, while I came to see it as oppression. He could peel back the layers of hypocrisy and intolerance and see what was good, and I couldn't. He believed that it mattered what he did in life, and he believed in the next world, one that's better. He kept the faith of his Mennonite forebears to the very end, or what he might call the beginning, and removed himself from this world entirely.

Stephanie, the waitress in the café in Woodridge, told my mother that my dad was calm and polite when he spoke to her, as if he were about to sit down to a cup of tea. She told her that he hadn't seemed at all afraid. But why would you be if you believed you were going to a place where there is no more sadness?

My dad never talked to us about God or religion. We didn't have family devotion like everybody else. He never quoted out loud from the Bible or lectured us about not going to church. In fact his only two pieces of advice to me were "Be yourself" and "You can do anything."

But he still went to church. It didn't matter how low he felt, or how cold it was outside. He would put on his suit and tie and stylish cap and walk the seven or eight blocks to church. He always walked, through searing heat or sub-arctic chill. If he was away on holidays he would find a church and go to it. At the lake he drove forty miles down gravel roads to attend an outdoor church in the bush. I think he needed church like a junkie needs a fix: to get him through another day in a world of pain.

What I love about my town is that it gave my dad the faith that stopped him from being afraid in those last violent seconds he spent on earth. And the place in my mind where we meet is on the front steps of my dad's church, the big one on Main Street across from Don's Bakery and the Goodwill store. We smile and talk for a few minutes outside, basking in the warmth of the summer sun he loved so much. Then he goes in and I stay outside, and we're both happy where we are.

—2001

ren Connelly

b. 1969

Karen Connelly is a Canadian writer known for her work in poetry, fiction, and non-fiction; she has received accolades in all three genres. Her first book, the collection of poetry *The Small Words in My Body* (1990), won the Pat Lowther Award for Best Book of Poetry in 1991. Her second book, *Touch the Dragon, A Thai Journal* (1992), received the Governor General's Award for English-language Non-fiction. *The Lizard Cage* (2005), her first novel, was awarded Britain's Orange Broadband Prize for New Fiction in 2007.

Connelly was born in Calgary, Alberta, into a working-class, fundamentalist Christian family. When she was 17, she received a Rotary scholarship to live in a small village in Thailand for a year. She returned to Canada, but soon turned down a number of university scholarships in favour of a life of travel and artistic pursuit in Spain and France. She spent her time honing her craft, recording her adventures, and organizing and refining the journals and letters that documented her time in Thailand. Those documents would eventually be shaped into *Touch the Dragon*; the selection here is an excerpt from that work.

Connelly's travels continued, eventually drawing her back to Thailand and, later, into Burma. Troubled by what she saw as the Orwellian dictatorship in Burma, Connelly took a more activist approach to her art; she was eventually blacklisted from travel to Burma for taking unauthorized photographs of a student demonstration. After her expulsion, she remained in Thailand and interviewed many Burmese dissidents, revolutionaries, and artists. These experiences led to the book of poetry *The Border Surrounds Us* (2000) and the novel *The Lizard Cage*. Connelly has written that she "grew up *believing* that the novel was a powerful act of creation; that books could change people's lives; that a brilliant novel, especially if it was brave enough to wade into politics, could constitute a kind of action, be a form of intervention."

from *Touch the Dragon: A Thai Journal*

August 21, 1986

Leaving Canada. A view of the body of mountains: deep sockets of aquamarine, blue veins slipping over cliff-sides, stone edges splintering from the earth like cracked bones.

When I think of the span of countries, when I run my fingers over the skin of a map, I get dizzy. I am too high up now—I should have glided into this journey on a boat. As the country pulls out from under me, I overturn like a glass on a yanked table-cloth, I spill. Land steadies people, holds them, even if they imagine they control it. Land owns and defines us. Without it, we become something else.

After refuelling in Kyoto, we are moving again, rising into another time zone, another time. These are the first pages of a new country. There's almost nothing to write yet because I know so little. I can't even imagine where I'm going. I am utterly alone, a small bit of dust blown into Asia's deep green eye. I lean against the glass and gaze down at an emerald flood, knowing I'll never be able to soak up such radiance. It's a colour I never knew I'd see, the astonishing canvas of a dream, undreamed.

At the airport in Bangkok, a bald foreigner lugs three gallons of water on his shoulder. He explains to suspicious customs officials that he has brought water from home because the water here is unsafe. There is laughter, a waving of dark arms and pale palms. I stumble through customs, crippled by luggage and jet lag. One English word rings out: taxi. The world is a wet braid of heat and flesh, glimpses of gold-studded teeth, shirts open to shining bellies, purple tattoos, wreaths of jasmine. Above the horde of cab-drivers looms a hand-painted sign warning all tourists to beware of thieves, illicit business deals, drugs and fake gems. The air slides over me thick as honey. I have never felt such tropical warmth before.

Then I see a cardboard sign with my name on it bobbing up in the crowd. Someone has come to get me. Someone has come to take me (farther) away.

August 22

We are driving northwards under black clouds, through darkness broken by lightning. I could believe now that the earth is flat, and its far edges are sparking flame. Rice fields, tree groves, gleaming oval ponds flash out of the night. Mr. Prasit Piyachinda and Mr. Prasert Jeenanukulwong have both suggested I call them *paw* for the sake of simplicity. Paw Prasit speaks English. "We will treat you like a daughter, and you will treat us like father." The Rotary Club of Denchai has almost twenty members. I can't pronounce any of their names. "You must learn to speak Thai very quickly," Paw Prasit explains. "It will not be difficult. No one in your family speaks English. You have no choice." He turns around to smile at me. He talks about spicy food, a famous Buddhist monk who is also a great fortune-teller, the school I will go to, the people who are anxious to meet me. When I ask why these people want to meet me, he giggles. "Why, because you are a falang." A foreigner. It is my first Thai word.

Sudden light spears the heavy rain. I squint out the streaming windows. The men laugh at my fascination with the countryside. "Are you afraid of the ... the ..."

"The lightning," I finish for Paw Prasit.

"Ah, yes, yes, are you afraid of it? My daughter, yes, is. She will not look at fields at night, fields in rain." He points towards a distant clump of trees and taps at the window. "Dragons. She says they are dragons." He laughs, turns to Prasert, translates, they laugh again, then hoot more at some other joke. I peer through the glass; his daughter is right. There they are, tree-dragons, moulded by wind and shadow, heavy-skulled dinosaurs gathered under lightning at the edges of ponds. They lean down to the water, their scaled flanks gleaming with rain.

I fall asleep, sliding down onto the seat, listening to Paw Prasit say, "And people will call you falang in the street because at first they will not know your name." I will be the only white person in the town. "You will be popular. Also there is a green fruit in Thailand called falang and when you eat it, everyone will laugh and say, 'Falang eat falang. Hahaha. Ha ha.'" Again he translates for Paw Prasert (why are their names so similar?) and both men slap their knees at this hilarious play on words. I keep missing the jokes in everything, possibly because I'm so tired. What time is it here? What time is it in Canada? Canada? The word sounds funny. I slump down farther on the seat and listen to wheels humming and my guardians speaking Thai. It is indecipherable birdsong. They talk on, their voices climbing and sliding down the banisters of five tones and strange letters. This is not comparable to high school French.

Suddenly, inexplicably, they are standing outside the car and calling me. "Kalen, Kalen, to bathroom now. We are in Phitsanulok. For pee-pee." The door is opened for me. I receive a handful of toilet paper and a gentle push in the right direction. I am disoriented, eyes salted with sleep. The young men hanging about the gas pumps stare and stare.

Once I am in the dark little washroom, reality swarms; the pungent odour of urine burns the dreamy quality out of everything. I lose my footing on the wet edges of the Thai toilet and laugh, imagining the embarrassment of breaking my ankle in a toilet the very first day. This is Thailand, the land of smiles, the Venice of the Orient, the pearl of Asia. The travel-agency phrases run off my tongue as mosquitoes settle on my thighs, arms, neck. Are they malarial or harmless? A few dark stains move up and down the walls, and my skin shivers, waiting for invasions.

Walking back across the lot, I notice small reddish lights glowing behind a cage with thin bars. I walk towards them, curious, moving closer, closer, stretching out my hand ... Paw Prasit yells, "No, no!" but it's too late. All I do is touch the bars and half a dozen gibbons leap shrieking towards my hand.

I scream at their screams, the gas-station attendants come loping across the lot and my Thai fathers rush forward to pull me away. I apologize to everyone.

The gibbons are the ones making the fuss. Their furious bodies spring and bounce inside the cage. "You must learn to be careful, Kalen." Paw Prasit takes my arm, his glasses steamed with worry. "There are snakes, too. You know?" He stares at me for a moment, then laughs and says something in Thai, which makes Paw Prasert laugh, too. Even the gas-pumpers giggle and kick a few pebbles, looking up at me even though their heads are lowered. I open the car door and crawl in. When we drive away, the boys wave us off. I stare back at the neon lights of the station for a long time, the savage human faces of the monkeys still vivid in my mind.

We reach Denchai in the dark, so I see little, other than dogs running through the beams of the headlights, barely making it. We finally stop at the last building on the street. "Liquor store," Paw Prasit says. "This is the liquor store of Paw Prasert. This is where you'll live." Prasert is already out of the car and up on a bench, stretching to press a door buzzer. As soon as his finger flexes, I hear barking and the rattling slap of a chain. The dog inside the building hurls against the metal door. We wait until the dog begins to whimper, then hear an old man's grunt and sniffle. There's a clatter of keys and a frightening roar of phlegm from the recesses of a throat; finally the door scrapes open along the cement floor. A balding old man beams at us. His skin is the colour and texture of a walnut, he is toothless and he wears nothing but a baggy pair of black satin trousers. Prasit says to me, "Old father is much blind." After awkward introductions, the three of them begin to speak in Thai. I smile and smile. Before coming in with us, the old man shuffles to the road and vigorously spits a small chunk of his lung into the gutter.

Inside the shop, the German shepherd once again begins to bark and strain against her chain. Her lips are pulled back over yellow teeth. Paw Prasert grins proudly, pulls up some long-forgotten vestige of English and yells over the barking, "My dog!" I smile back, nod. Paw Prasit adds, "But no worry, it not hurt you." She leaps toward us again, only to be choked back by the chain. After the old man hits her on the nose, she whimpers and slumps to the ground, chin between her paws. We walk deeper into the liquor store, past piles of dusty crates, a display of Thai whisky, a television, an old desk piled with newspapers and small bags of rice. Each of the men has one of my suitcases and is breathing audibly under its weight, insisting how light it is. We come to a small fridge. Paw Prasert opens it and whispers to Paw Prasit, who turns to me. "He say you take anything you want, you are like a daughter to him. You know?"

Thanking them, I glance into the fridge. It's full of water bottles and a few pots of murky sauces or oil paints.

Up one staircase: bathroom, sister's room, children's room. Paw Prasert's room. The top of another staircase brings us to an uninhabited floor. The one bedroom is for me. "You have room all to self." I am smiling, smiling my thanks. Now the men turn to leave. Yes, yes, see you tomorrow, to begin learning Thai, to begin learning, tomorrow, yes.

And the door closes. I look around: a low bed of cushions, a child's desk, a small mirror, a woven straw chair. Green curtains, green bedspread. A stark naked Thai girl with an erotic smile stares down from a picture on the wall. This smile—she must be kidding—does the trick. I sit on the edge of the bed, hug my elbows and sob for everything that isn't here. I think of the hundreds of days, the thousands of hours I have to stay here. Everything I understand, everything I own is buried in my skull, intangible. I am not feeling particularly brave. I'm sniffling, alone but for a Thai porn queen and three beaten-up suitcases. This does not feel exotic. Around me, the pool of night trembles with crickets and frogs, breaks with the distant bark of dogs, and slowly, slowly, closes over my head.

—1993

Glossary

Aesthetes: members of a late nineteenth-century movement that valued "art for art's sake"—for its purely aesthetic qualities, as opposed to valuing art for the moral content it may convey, for the intellectual stimulation it may provide, or for a range of other qualities.

Allegory: a narrative with both a literal meaning and secondary, often symbolic meaning or meanings. Allegory frequently employs personification to give concrete embodiment to abstract concepts or entities, such as feelings or personal qualities. It may also present one set of characters or events in the guise of another, using implied parallels for the purposes of satire or political comment.

Alliteration: the grouping of words with the same initial consonant (e.g., "break, blow, burn, and make me new"). See also *assonance* and *consonance*.

Allusion: a reference, often indirect or unidentified, to a person, thing, or event. A reference in one literary work to another literary work, whether to its content or its form, also constitutes an allusion.

Ambiguity: an "opening" of language created by the writer to allow for multiple meanings or differing interpretations. In literature, ambiguity may be deliberately employed by the writer to enrich meaning; this differs from any unintentional, unwanted ambiguity in non-literary prose.

Anachronism: accidentally or intentionally attributing people, things, ideas, and events to historical periods in which they do not and could not possibly belong.

Analogy: a broad term that refers to our processes of noting similarities among things or events. Specific forms of analogy include *simile* and *metaphor*.

Apostrophe: a figure of speech (a *trope*; see *figures of speech*) in which a writer directly addresses an object—or a dead or absent person—as if the imagined audience were actually listening.

Archetype: in literature and mythology, a recurring idea, symbol, motif, character, or place. To some scholars and psychologists, an archetype represents universal human thought-patterns or experiences.

Assonance: the repetition of identical or similar vowel sounds in stressed syllables in which the surrounding consonants are different: for example, "shame" and "fate"; "gale" and "cage"; or the long "i" sounds in "Beside the pumice isle...."

Atmosphere: see *tone*.

Baroque: powerful and heavily ornamented in style. "Baroque" is a term from the history of visual art and of music that is sometimes also used to describe certain literary styles.

Bathos: an anticlimactic effect brought about by a writer's descent from an elevated subject or tone to the ordinary or trivial.

Black Comedy: humour based on death, horror, or any incongruously macabre subject matter.

Bombast: inappropriately inflated or grandiose language.

Burlesque: satire of a particularly exaggerated sort, particularly that which ridicules its subject by emphasizing its vulgar or ridiculous aspects.

Canon: in literature, those works that are commonly accepted as possessing authority or importance. In practice, "canonical" texts or authors are those that are discussed most frequently by scholars and taught most frequently in university courses.

Caricature: an exaggerated and simplified depiction of character; the reduction of a personality to one or two telling traits at the expense of all other nuances and contradictions.

Characterization: the means by which an author develops and presents a character's personality qualities and distinguishing traits. A character may be established in the story by descriptive commentary or may be developed less directly—for example, through his or her words, actions, thoughts, and interactions with other characters.

Chiasmus: a figure of speech (a scheme) that reverses word order in successive parallel clauses. If the word order is A-B-C in the first clause, it becomes C-B-A in the second: for example, Donne's line "She is all states, and all princes, I" ("The Sun Rising") incorporates this reversal.

Classical: originating in or relating to ancient Greek or Roman culture. As commonly conceived, *classical* implies a strong sense of formal order. The term *neoclassical* is often used with reference to literature of the Restoration and eighteenth century that was strongly influenced by ancient Greek and Roman models.

Conflict: struggles between characters and opposing forces. Conflict can be internal (psychological) or external (conflict with another character, for instance, or with society or nature).

Connotation: the implied, often unspoken meaning(s) of a given word, as distinct from its *denotation*, or literal meaning. Connotations may have highly emotional undertones and are usually culturally specific.

Convention: aesthetic approach, technique, or practice accepted as characteristic and appropriate for a particular form. It is a convention of certain sorts of plays, for example, that the characters speak in blank verse, of other sorts of plays that characters speak in rhymed couplets, and of still other sorts of dramatic performances that characters frequently break into song to express their feelings.

Denotation: see *connotation*.

Dialogue: words spoken by characters to one another. (When a character is addressing him or her self or the audience directly, the words spoken are referred to as a "soliloquy.")

Diction: word choice. Whether the diction of a literary work (or of a literary character) is colloquial, conversational, formal, or of some other type contributes significantly to the tone of the text as well as to characterization.

Didacticism: aesthetic approach emphasizing moral instruction.

Dramatic Irony: this form of *irony* occurs when an audience has access to information not available to the character.

Ellipsis: the omission of a word or words necessary for the complete grammatical construction of a sentence, but not necessary for our understanding of the sentence.

Epic Simile: an elaborate simile, developed at such length that the vehicle of the comparison momentarily displaces the primary subject with which it is being compared.

Epigraph: a quotation placed at the beginning of a work to indicate or foreshadow the theme.

Epiphany: a moment at which matters of significance are suddenly illuminated for a literary character (or for the reader), typically triggered by something small and seemingly of little import. The term first came into wide currency in connection with the fiction of James Joyce.

Ethos: the perceived character, trustworthiness, or credibility of a writer or narrator.

Eulogy: text expressing praise, especially for a distinguished person recently deceased.

Euphemism: mode of expression through which aspects of reality considered to be vulgar, crudely physical, or unpleasant are referred to indirectly rather than named explicitly. A variety of euphemisms exist for the processes of urination and defecation; *passed away* is often used as a euphemism for *died*.

Existentialism: a philosophical approach according to which the meaning of human life is derived from the actual experience of the living individual. The existential worldview, in which life is assumed to have no essential or pre-existing meanings other than those we personally choose to endow it with, can produce an *absurdist* sensibility.

Exposition: the setting out of material in an ordered (and usually concise) form, either in speech or in writing. In a play those parts of the action that do not occur on stage but are rather recounted by the characters are frequently described as being presented in exposition. Similarly, when the background narrative is filled in near the beginning of a novel, such material is often described as having been presented in exposition.

Fiction: imagined or invented narrative. In literature, the term is usually used to refer to prose narratives (such as novels and short stories).

Figures of Speech: deliberate, highly concentrated uses of language to achieve particular purposes or effects on an audience. There are two kinds of figures: schemes and *tropes*. Schemes involve changes in word-sound and word-order, such as *alliteration* and *chiasmus*. Tropes play on our understandings of words to extend, alter, or transform meaning, as in *metaphor* and *personification*.

First-Person Narrative: narrative recounted using *I* and *me*. See also *narrative perspective*.

Flashback: the inclusion in the primary thread of a story's narrative of a scene (or scenes) from an earlier point in time. Flashbacks may be used to revisit from a different viewpoint events that have already been recounted in the main thread of narrative; to present material that has been left out in the initial recounting; or to present relevant material from a time before the beginning of the main thread of narrative. The use of flashbacks is sometimes referred to as "analepsis."

Flashforward: the inclusion in the primary thread of a story's narrative of a scene (or scenes) from a later point in time.

Flat Character: the opposite of a *round character*, a flat character is defined by a small number of traits and does not possess enough complexity to be psychologically realistic. "Flat character" can be a disparaging term, but need not be; flat characters serve different purposes in a fiction than round characters, and are often better suited to some types of literature, such as allegory or farcical comedy.

Foil: in literature, a character whose behaviour and/or qualities set in relief for the reader or audience those of a strongly contrasting character who plays a more central part in the story.

Foreshadowing: the inclusion of elements in a story that hint at some later development(s) in the same story.

Freytag's Pyramid: a model of plot structure developed by the German novelist, playwright, and critic Gustav Freytag and introduced in his book *Die Technik des Dramas* (1863). In the pyramid, five stages of plot are identified as occurring in the following order: exposition, rising action, climax, falling action, and "dénouement." Freytag intended his pyramid to diagram the structure of classical five-act plays, but it is also used as a tool to analyze other forms of fiction (even though many individual plays and stories do not follow the structure outlined in the pyramid).

Genre: a class or type of literary work. The concept of genre may be used with different levels of generality. At the most general, poetry, drama, and prose fiction are distinguished as separate genres. At a lower level of generality various sub-genres are frequently distinguished, such as (within the genre of prose fiction) the novel, the novella, and the short story; and, at a still lower level of generality, the mystery novel, the detective novel, the novel of manners, and so on.

Gothic: in architecture and the visual arts, a term used to describe styles prevalent from the twelfth to the fourteenth centuries, but in literature a term used to describe work with a sinister or grotesque tone that seeks to evoke a sense of terror on the part of the reader or audience. Gothic literature originated as a genre in the eighteenth century with works such as Horace Walpole's *The Castle of Otranto*. To some extent the notion of the medieval itself then carried with it associations of the dark and the grotesque, but from the beginning an element of intentional exaggeration (sometimes verging on self-parody) attached itself to the genre. The Gothic trend of youth culture that began in the late twentieth century is less clearly associated with the medieval, but shares with the various varieties of Gothic literature (from Walpole in the eighteenth century, to Bram Stoker in the early twentieth, to Stephen King and Anne Rice in the late twentieth) a fondness for the sensational and the grotesque, as well as a propensity to self-parody.

Grotesque: literature of the grotesque is characterized by a focus on extreme or distorted aspects of human characteristics. (The term can also refer particularly to a character who is odd or disturbing.) This focus can serve to comment on and challenge societal norms. The story "A Good Man Is Hard to Find" employs elements of the grotesque.

Hyperbole: a *figure of speech* (a *trope*) that deliberately exaggerates or inflates meaning to achieve particular effects, such as the irony in A.E. Housman's claim (from "Terence, This Is Stupid Stuff") that "malt does more than Milton can / To justify God's ways to man."

Image: a representation of a sensory experience or of an object that can be known by the senses.

Imagery: the range of images in a given work. We can gain much insight into works by looking for patterns of imagery.

Intertextuality: the relationships between one literary work and other literary works. A literary work may connect with other works through *allusion*, *parody*, or *satire*, or in a variety of other ways.

Irony: the use of irony draws attention to a gap between what is said and what is meant, or what appears to be true and what is true. Types of irony include verbal irony (which includes *hyberbole*, *litotes*, and *sarcasm*), *dramatic* *irony*, and structural irony (in which the gap between what is "said" and meant is sustained throughout an entire piece, as when an author makes use of an unreliable narrator or speaker—see Robert Browning's "My Last Duchess").

Litotes: a *figure of speech* (a *trope*) in which a writer deliberately uses understatement to highlight the importance of an argument, or to convey an ironic attitude.

Metaphor: a *figure of speech* (in this case, a *trope*) in which a comparison is made or identity is asserted between two unrelated things or actions without the use of "like" or "as."

Metonymy: a *figure of speech* (a *trope*), meaning "change of name," in which a writer refers to an object or idea by substituting the name of another object or idea closely associated with it: for example, the substitution of "crown" for monarchy, "the press" for journalism, or "the pen" for writing. *Synecdoche* is a kind of metonymy.

Modernism: in the history of literature, music, and the visual arts, a movement that began in the early twentieth century, characterized by a thoroughgoing rejection of the then-dominant conventions of literary plotting and characterization, of melody and harmony, and of perspective and other naturalistic forms of visual representation. In literature (as in music and the visual arts), modernists endeavoured to represent the complexity of what seemed to them to be an increasingly fragmented world by adopting techniques of presenting story material, illuminating character, and employing imagery that emphasized (in the words of Virginia Woolf) "the spasmodic, the obscure, the fragmentary."

Monologue: an extended speech by a single speaker or character in a poem or play.

Mood: this can describe the writer's attitude, implied or expressed, toward the subject (see *tone*); or it may refer to the atmosphere that a writer creates in a passage of description or narration.

Motif: pattern formed by the recurrence of an idea, image, action, or plot element throughout a literary work, creating new levels of meaning and strengthening structural coherence. The term is taken from music, where it describes recurring melodies or themes. See also *theme*.

Narration: the process of disclosing information, whether fictional or non-fictional.

Narrative Perspective: in fiction, the point of view from which a story is narrated. A first-person narrative is recounted using *I* and *me*, whereas a third-person narrative is recounted using *he, she, they*, and so on. When a narrative is written in the third person and the narrative voice evidently "knows" all that is being done and thought, the story is typically described as being recounted by an "omniscient narrator." Second-person narratives, in which the narrative is recounted using *you*, are very rare.

Narrator: the voice (or voices) disclosing information. In fiction, the narrator is distinguished from both the author (a real, historical person) and the implied author (whom the reader imagines the author to be). Narrators can also be distinguished according to the degree to which they share the reality of the other characters in the story and the extent to which they participate in the action; according to how much information they are privy to (and how much of that information they are willing to share with the reader); and according to whether or not they are perceived by the reader as reliable or unreliable sources of information. See also *narrative perspective*.

Neoclassicism: literally the "new classicism," the aesthetic style that dominated high culture in Europe through the seventeenth and eighteenth centuries, and in some places into the nineteenth century. Its subject matter was often taken from Greek and Roman myth and history; in *style*, it valued order, reason, clarity, and moderation.

Omniscient Narrator: see *narrative perspective*.

Oxymoron: a *figure of speech* (a *trope*) in which two words whose meanings seem contradictory are placed together; we see an example in Shakespeare's *Twelfth Night*, when Orsino refers to the "sweet pangs" of love.

Parody: a close, usually mocking imitation of a particular literary work, or of the well-known style of a particular author, in order to expose or magnify weaknesses. Parody is a form of *satire*—that is, humour that may ridicule and scorn its object.

Pastiche: a discourse that borrows or imitates other writers' characters, forms, style, or ideas, sometimes creating something of a literary patchwork. Unlike a parody, a pastiche can be intended as a compliment to the original writer.

Pathetic Fallacy: a form of *personification* in which inanimate objects are given human emotions: for example, rain clouds "weeping." The word "fallacy" in this connection is intended to suggest the distortion of reality or the false emotion that may result from an exaggerated use of personification.

Pathos: the emotional quality of a discourse; or the ability of a discourse to appeal to our emotions. It is usually applied to the mood conveyed by images of pain, suffering, or loss that arouse feelings of pity or sorrow in the reader.

Persona: the assumed identity or "speaking voice" that a writer projects in a discourse. The term "persona" literally means "mask."

Personification: a *figure of speech* (a *trope*), also known as "prosopopoeia," in which a writer refers to inanimate objects, ideas, or non-human animals as if they were human, or creates a human figure to represent an abstract entity such as Philosophy or Peace.

Plot: the organization of story materials within a literary work. Matters of plotting include the order in which story material is presented; the inclusion of elements that allow or encourage the reader or audience to form expectations as to what is likely to happen; and the decision to present some story material through exposition rather than present it directly to the reader as part of the narrative.

Point of View: see *narrative perspective.*

Postmodernism: in literature and the visual arts, a movement influential in the late twentieth and early twenty-first centuries. In some ways postmodernism represents a reaction to modernism, in others an extension of it. With roots in the work of French philosophers such as Jacques Derrida and Michel Foucault, it is deeply coloured by theory; indeed, it may be said to have begun at the "meta" level of theorizing rather than at the level of practice. Like modernism, postmodernism embraces difficulty and distrusts the simple and straightforward. More broadly, postmodernism is characterized by a rejection of absolute truth or value, of closed systems, of grand unified narratives.

Postmodernist fiction is characterized by a frequently ironic or playful tone in dealing with reality and illusion; by a willingness to combine different styles or forms in a single work (just as in architecture the postmodernist spirit embodies a willingness to borrow from seemingly disparate styles in designing a single structure); and by a highly attuned awareness of the problematized state of the writer, artist, or theorist as observer.

Protagonist: the central character in a literary work.

Pun: a play on words, in which a word with two or more distinct meanings, or two words with similar sounds, may create humorous ambiguities. Also known as "paranomasia."

Realism: as a literary term, the presentation through literature of material closely resembling real life. As notions both of what constitutes "real life" and of how it may be most faithfully represented in literature have varied widely, "realism" has taken a variety of meanings. The term "naturalistic" has sometimes been used as a synonym for *realistic*; naturalism originated in the nineteenth century as a term denoting a form of realism focusing in particular on grim, unpleasant, or ugly aspects of the real.

Rhetoric: in classical Greece and Rome, the art of persuasion and public speaking. From the Middle Ages onwards, the study of rhetoric gave greater attention to style, particularly *figures of speech*. Today in poetics, the term rhetoric may encompass not only figures of speech, but also the persuasive effects of forms, sounds, and word choices.

Romanticism: a major social and cultural movement, originating in Europe, that shaped much of Western artistic thought in the late eighteenth and nineteenth centuries. Opposing the ideal of controlled, rational order associated with the Enlightenment, Romanticism emphasizes the importance of spontaneous self-expression, emotion, and personal experience in producing art. In Romanticism, the "natural" is privileged over the conventional or the artificial.

Round Character: a complex and psychologically realistic character, often one who changes as a work progresses. The opposite of a round character is a *flat character*.

Sarcasm: a form of *irony* (usually spoken) in which the meaning is conveyed largely by the tone of voice adopted; something said sarcastically is meant to imply its opposite.

Satire: literary work designed to make fun of or seriously criticize its subject. According to many literary theories of the Renaissance and neoclassical periods, the ridicule through satire of a certain sort of behaviour may function for the reader or audience as a corrective of such behaviour.

Scheme: see *figures of speech*.

Setting: the time, place, and cultural environment in which a story or work takes place.

Simile: a *figure of speech* (a *trope*) which makes an explicit comparison between a particular object and another object or idea that is similar in some (often unexpected) way. A simile always uses "like" or "as" to signal the connection. Compare with *metaphor*.

Stock Character: a character defined by a set of characteristics that are stereotypical and/or established by literary convention; examples include the "wicked stepmother" and the "absent-minded professor."

Story: narrative material, independent of the manner in which it may be presented or the ways in which the narrative material may be organized. Story is thus distinct from *plot*.

Stream of Consciousness: a narrative technique that conveys the inner workings of a character's mind, in which a character's thoughts, feelings, memories, and impressions are related in an unbroken flow, without concern for chronology or coherence.

Style: a distinctive or specific use of language and form.

Subtext: implied or suggested meaning of a passage of text, or of an entire work.

Surrealism: Surrealism incorporates elements of the true appearance of life and nature, combining these elements according to a logic more typical of dreams than waking life. Isolated aspects of surrealist art may create powerful illusions of reality, but the effect of the whole is usually to disturb or question our sense of reality rather than to confirm it.

Symbol: something that represents itself but goes beyond this in suggesting other meanings. Like metaphor, the symbol extends meaning; but while the tenor and vehicle of metaphor are bound in a specific relationship, a symbol may have a range of connotations. For example, the image of a rose may call forth associations of love, passion, transience, fragility, youth, and beauty, among others. Depending upon the context, such an image could be interpreted in a variety of ways, as in Blake's lyric, "The Sick Rose."

Synecdoche: a kind of *metonymy* in which a writer substitutes the name of a part of something to signify the whole: for example, "sail" for ship or "hand" for a member of the ship's crew.

Syntax: the ordering of words in a sentence.

Theme: in general, an idea explored in a work through character, action, and/ or image. To be fully developed, however, a theme must consist of more than a single concept or idea: it should also include an argument about the idea. Thus if a poem examines the topic of jealousy, we might say the theme is that jealousy undermines love or jealousy is a manifestation of insecurity. Few, if any, literary works have single themes.

Third-Person Narrative: see *narrative perspective*.

Tone: the writer's attitude toward a given subject or audience, as expressed through an authorial persona or "voice." Tone can be projected through particular choices of wording, imagery, figures of speech, and rhythmic devices. Compare *mood*.

Tragedy: in the traditional definition originating in discussions of ancient Greek drama, a serious narrative recounting the downfall of the protagonist, usually a person of high social standing. More loosely, the term has been applied to a wide variety of literary forms in which the tone is predominantly a dark one and the narrative does not end happily.

Trope: any figure of speech that plays on our understandings of words to extend, alter, or transform "literal" meaning. Common tropes include *metaphor, simile, personification, hyperbole, metonymy, oxymoron, synecdoche*, and *irony*. See also *figures of speech*.

Zeugma: a *figure of speech* (*trope*) in which one word links or "yokes" two others in the same sentence, often to comic or ironic effect. For example, a verb may govern two objects, as in Pope's line "Or stain her honour, or her new brocade."

Permission Acknowledgements

Please note that texts in the public domain do not appear in the list below and that all introductory materials and annotations in this volume are copyright © Broadview Press.

Roland Barthes. "The World of Wrestling," from *Mythologies* by Roland Barthes, published by Vintage Books. Reprinted by permission of The Random House Group Limited.

Karen Connelly. Entries for August 21 and 22 from *Touch the Dragon: A Thai Journal*. Turnstone Press, 1992, 2010. Reprinted with the permission of Karen Connelly.

Philip Gourevitch. Excerpt from *We Wish to Inform You That Tomorrow We Will Be Killed with Our Families* by Philip Gourevitch. Copyright © 1998 by Philip Gourevitch. Reprinted by permission of Farrar, Straus and Giroux, LLC.

Drew Hayden Taylor. "Pretty Like a White Boy," Introduction from *Funny, You Don't Look Like One: Observations of A Blue-Eyed Ojibway* (revised edition). Theytus Books, 1998. Copyright © Drew Hayden Taylor. Reprinted with the permission of the author and Aurora Artists Incorporated.

Miriam Toews. "A Father's Faith," first published in *Saturday Night Magazine*. Copyright © 1999 by Miriam Toews. Used by permission of The Wylie Agency, LLC.

David Foster Wallace. "Consider the Lobster," originally published in *Gourmet Magazine*, 2004. Copyright © 2005, David Foster Wallace, *Consider the Lobster and Other Essays*, Little, Brown and Company. Used by permission of the David Foster Wallace Literary Trust.

The publisher has endeavoured to contact rights holders for all copyrighted material, and would appreciate receiving any information as to errors or omissions.

Index of Authors and Titles

from the publisher

A name never says it all, but the word "broadview" expresses a good deal of the philosophy behind our company. We are open to a broad range of academic approaches and political viewpoints. We pay attention to the broad impact book publishing and book printing has in the wider world; we began using recycled stock more than a decade ago, and for some years now we have used 100% recycled paper for most titles. As a Canadian-based company we naturally publish a number of titles with a Canadian emphasis, but our publishing program overall is internationally oriented and broad-ranging. Our individual titles often appeal to a broad readership too; many are of interest as much to general readers as to academics and students.

Founded in 1985, Broadview remains a fully independent company owned by its shareholders—not an imprint or subsidiary of a larger multinational.

If you would like to find out more about Broadview and about the books we publish, please visit us at **www.broadviewpress.com**. And if you'd like to place an order through the site, we'd like to show our appreciation by extending a special discount to you: by entering the code below you will receive a 20% discount on purchases made through the Broadview website.

Discount code: **broadview20%**

Thank you for choosing Broadview.

Please note: this offer applies only to sales of bound books within the United States or Canada.

LIST

of products used:

741 lb(s) of Rolland Enviro100 Print
100% post-consumer

RESULTS

Based on the Cascades products you selected
compared to products in the industry made with
100% virgin fiber, your savings are:

 6 trees

 6,130 gal. US of water
66 days of water consumption

 775 lbs of waste
7 waste containers

 2,014 lbs CO2
3,820 miles driven

 10 MMBTU
47,775 60W light bulbs for one hour

 6 lbs NOx
**emissions of one truck during 8
days**